Kansas Legal Research

Kansas Legal Research

Joseph A. Custer

Christopher L. Steadham

Suzanne E. Rowe, Series Editor

CAROLINA ACADEMIC PRESS

Durham, North Carolina

Library of Congress Cataloging-in-Publication Data

Custer, Joseph A., 1960-
  Kansas legal research / Joseph A. Custer, Christopher L. Steadham.
    p. cm.
  Includes bibliographical references and index.
  ISBN 978-1-59460-509-3 (alk. paper)
  1. Legal research--Kansas. I. Steadham, Christopher. II. Title.
KFK75.C87 2008
340.072'0781--dc22

                                                        2008029216

CAROLINA ACADEMIC PRESS
700 Kent Street
Durham, North Carolina 27701
Telephone (919) 489-7486
Fax (919) 493-5668
www.cap-press.com

Printed in the United States of America.

For Kaitlyn and Ben.
You're the bomb!
Love, Dad

JAC

To my parents — my constant source of inspiration.

CLS

Summary of Contents

Contents

List of Tables and Figures

Series Note

The Legal Research Series published by Carolina Academic Press includes an increasing number of titles from states around the country. The goal of each book is to provide law students, practitioners, paralegals, college students, laypeople, and librarians with the essential elements of legal research in each state. Unlike more bibliographic texts, the Legal Research Series books seek to explain concisely both the sources of state law research and the process for conducting legal research effectively.

Foreword

Steve Leben

Judge, Kansas Court of Appeals

When students near the end of their education, they often turn their attention to the interests of employers. My advice to them about what employers look for from lawyers is often quite simple. Employers want people who can figure out quickly what key questions will actually determine the outcome, who can find the key cases and concepts that will shape the answers, and who can write an effective summary and analysis of that information. Good legal research skills are at the heart of it all.

So I was delighted when Joe Custer and Chris Steadham told me that they were writing this book. Getting students started doing research the right way is critical.

I was even more pleased when I saw the book. It takes the process of legal research in Kansas law and gives it structure. Readers will know how to plan a successful research project, and they will know how to make sure that nothing of significance has been overlooked. This will be of great benefit to students and practitioners alike.

The book does more, though, than tell you how to plan your research project. It also takes you through *Kansas-specific* resources. Every state has its quirks, and Kansas is no different. Custer and Steadham provide the background you need to research the Kansas Constitution, Kansas statutes, and Kansas caselaw. And they are very thorough.

I had two acid tests in mind when I looked at this book. First, I looked to see whether the authors gave an appropriate nod to the most important—and most frequently overlooked—rule in statu-

tory interpretation: *start by reading the whole statute carefully.* Given
the vast reach of statutes in modern America, statutory research skills
are critical. And Custer and Steadham got it right, noting that the
"most important step" is the most basic one: *"Read the statute very
carefully."* As they noted, "[F]ew statutes are so clear that they can be
understood on one reading." Researchers often try to avoid the hard
work of parsing the words in a statute by looking for guidance from
caselaw. Sometimes they find a case on point but overlook a later
statutory amendment that makes the case irrelevant. Those who follow the steps set out in this book will not make that mistake.

Second, I looked to see whether the authors acknowledged the vast
resource on Kansas law available in the unpublished opinions of the
Kansas state and federal courts. Once again, they got it right. Researchers who know to check for those unpublished opinions have a
big advantage over those who aren't aware of them. My own court
decides more than 1,300 cases each year, but publishes only 10% to
15% of them. Every week, I find helpful research in the unpublished
opinions of my court, the Kansas Supreme Court, and the Kansas
federal courts.

This book, then, will surely get the newcomer to legal research ori-
ented to the task of Kansas legal research. But it will also be of great
help to the practitioner. It includes Kansas-specific background material and research techniques that will help anyone who has ever
struggled with a research project; it will also help provide a refresher
course of up-to-date techniques to those whose research skills were
honed—well, let's just say more than a few years ago. Kansas lawyers
should take the time to review it, and most would be wise to keep a
copy nearby.

The Kansas legal community has gained from the publication of
this book.

Preface and Acknowledgments

The primary audience for this book includes first-year law students enrolled in a course that integrates hands-on research with legal analysis and writing, as well as law students in upper-level legal research courses. Other audiences include attorneys, law librarians, paralegals, college students, and pro se litigants.

We are greatly indebted to Suzanne E. Rowe, editor of the Carolina Academic Press Legal Research Series, for her patient and meticulous editing. In addition, chapters on the research process, citators, online research, and strategies and portions of other discussions are drawn from her excellent publication, *Oregon Legal Research, Second Edition*. Suzanne's guidance was invaluable in the creation of this publication.

Kansas Court of Appeals Judge Steve Leben offered many valuable insights, especially those regarding the increasing importance of unpublished opinions. Most of our wonderful colleagues at the Wheat Law Library contributed time and effort to this project in some capacity. Katherine Greene, Jeff Montgomery, Allison Reeve, Gale Troth, Pamela Tull, and Lauren Van Waardhuizen were exceptionally helpful in this regard. Research assistants Sara Buffie, Kelly Fahl, Laura Koths, Kaitlan Monroe, and Daniel Moskowitz provided outstanding support at various stages of the writing process. We are also exceedingly grateful to all of our friends and colleagues at the University of Kansas School of Law for providing the collegial academic environment that allowed this project to flourish.

Joseph A. Custer
Christopher L. Steadham
June 2008

xxv

Kansas Legal Research

Chapter 1

The Research Process and Legal Analysis

I. Kansas Legal Research

The fundamentals of legal research are the same in every American jurisdiction, though the details vary. While some variations are minor, others require specialized knowledge of the resources available and the analytical framework in which those resources are used. This book focuses on the resources and analysis required to be thorough and effective in researching Kansas law. It supplements this focus with brief explanations of federal research and research into the law of other states, both to introduce other resources and to highlight some of the variations.

II. The Intersection of Legal Research and Legal Analysis

The basic process of legal research is simple. For most print resources, you will begin with an index, find entries that appear relevant, read those sections of the text, and then find out whether more recent information is available. For most online research, you will search particular websites or databases using words likely to appear in the text of relevant documents.

Legal analysis is interwoven throughout this process, raising challenging questions. In print research, which words will you look up in the index? How will you decide whether an index entry looks promising? With online research, how will you choose relevant words and construct a search most likely to produce the documents you need? When you read the text of a document, how will you determine whether it is relevant to your client's situation? How will you learn whether more recent material changed the law or merely applied it in a new situation? The answer to each of these questions requires legal analysis. This intersection of research and analysis can make legal research very difficult, especially for the novice. While this book's focus is legal research, it also includes the fundamental aspects of legal analysis required to conduct research competently.

This book is not designed to be a blueprint of every resource in the law library or search engine on the Internet; many resources contain their own detailed explanations in a preface or a "Help" section. This book is more like a manual or field guide, introducing the resources needed at each step of the research process and explaining how to use them.

III. Types of Legal Authority

Before researching the law, you must be clear about the goal of your search. In every research situation, you will want to find constitutional provisions, statutes, administrative rules, and judicial opinions that control your client's situation. In other words, you are searching for primary, mandatory authority.

Law is often divided along two lines. The first line distinguishes primary authority from secondary authority. *Primary authority* is law produced by government bodies with law-making power. Legislatures write statutes; courts write judicial opinions; and administrative agencies write rules (also called regulations). *Secondary authorities*, in contrast, are materials that are written about the law, generally by practicing attorneys, law professors, or legal editors. Secondary authorities include law practice guides, treatises, law review articles, and

Table 1-1. Examples of Authority in Kansas Research

	Mandatory Authority	Persuasive Authority
Primary Authority	Kansas statutes Kansas Supreme Court cases	Colorado statutes Missouri Supreme Court cases
Secondary Authority	—	Law review articles Legal encyclopedias

legal encyclopedias. These secondary sources are designed to aid you in understanding the law and locating primary authority.

Another division is made between mandatory and persuasive authority. *Mandatory authority* is binding on the court that would decide a conflict if the situation were litigated. In a question of Kansas law, mandatory or binding authority includes the Kansas Constitution, statutes enacted by the Kansas Legislature, opinions of the Supreme Court of Kansas,[1] and Kansas administrative rules. *Persuasive authority* is not binding, but may be followed if relevant and well reasoned. Authority may be merely persuasive if it is from a different jurisdiction or if it is not produced by a law-making body. In a question of Kansas law, examples of persuasive authority include a similar Colorado statute, an opinion of a Missouri state court, and a law review article. Notice in Table 1-1 that persuasive authority may be either primary or secondary authority, while mandatory authority is always primary.

Within primary, mandatory authority, there is an interlocking hierarchy of law involving constitutions, statutes, administrative rules, and judicial opinions. The constitution of each state is the supreme law of that state. If a statute is on point, that statute comes next in the hierarchy, followed by any relevant administrative rule. Judicial opinions may interpret the statute or rule, but they cannot disregard it. A judicial opinion may, however, decide that a statute violates the con-

---

1. Opinions from the Kansas Court of Appeals are binding on lower courts but not the Supreme Court of Kansas.

stitution or that a rule oversteps its bounds. If there is no constitutional provision, statute, or administrative rule on point, the issue will be controlled by *common law*, also called judge-made law or case law.[2]

IV. Overview of the Research Process

Conducting effective legal research means following a process. This process leads to the authority that controls a legal issue as well as to commentary that may help you analyze new and complex legal matters. The outline in Table 1-2 presents the basic research process.

This basic process should be customized for each research project. Consider whether you need to follow all seven steps, and if so, in what order. If you are unfamiliar with an area of law, you should follow each step of the process in the order indicated. Beginning with secondary sources will provide both context for the issues you must research and citations to relevant primary authority. As you gain experience in researching legal questions, you may choose to modify the process. For example, if you know that a situation is controlled by a statute, you may choose to begin with that step.

A. Getting Started

1. Gathering Facts and Determining Jurisdiction

The first step in any research process is to gather the facts of the client's situation. In law practice, gathering facts may include interviewing the client, reviewing documents, and talking to colleagues who are also working for the client.

An early question that arises for any research project is which jurisdiction's law controls. This book assumes that the client's situation is controlled by Kansas law, but you must determine whether federal law, the law of another state, tribal law, or local law is binding.

---

2. Common law is derived from judicial decisions, rather than statutes or constitutions. *Black's Law Dictionary* 293 (Bryan A. Garner, ed., 8th ed., West 2004).

Table 1-2. Overview of the Research Process

1. Gather facts, decide which jurisdiction controls, and *generate a list of research terms.*
2. Consult *secondary authorities* such as practice guides, treatises, legal encyclopedias, and law review articles. Secondary authorities explain the law and refer to primary authorities.
3. Find controlling *constitutional provisions, statutes,* or *rules* by reviewing their indexes or searching online for your research terms. Read these primary authorities carefully, update them if necessary, and then study their annotations for cross-references to additional authorities and explanatory materials.
4. Find citations to *cases* by searching *digests* or *online databases.* A digest is essentially a multi-volume topic index of cases in a certain jurisdiction or subject area.
5. Read the cases either in *reporters* or online. A reporter series publishes the full text of cases in a certain jurisdiction or subject area.
6. *Update* legal authorities by using a citator such as Shepard's or KeyCite to (a) ensure that an authority is still respected and (b) find additional sources that may be relevant to the research project.
7. *End* your research when you have no holes in your analysis and when you begin seeing the same authorities repeatedly.

2. Generating Research Terms

After gathering facts and determining the jurisdiction, generate a list of research terms. Many legal resources in print use lengthy indexes as the starting point for finding legal authority. Electronic sources often require the researcher to enter words that are likely to appear in a synopsis or in the full text of relevant documents. To ensure you are thorough in beginning a research project, you will need a comprehensive list of words, terms, and phrases that may lead to law on point. These may be legal terms or common words that describe the client's situation. The items on this list are *research terms.*

Organized brainstorming is the best way to compile a comprehensive list of research terms. Some researchers ask the journalistic questions: Who? What? How? Why? When? Where? Others use a mnemonic device like TARPP, which stands for Things, Actions, Remedies, People, and Places.[3] Whether you use one of these suggestions or develop your own method, generate a broad range of research terms regarding the facts, issues, and desired solutions of your client's situation. Include in the list both specific and general words. Try to think of synonyms and antonyms for each term since at this point you are uncertain which terms an index may include. Using a legal dictionary or thesaurus may generate additional terms.

As an example, assume you are working for a defense attorney who was recently assigned to a burglary case. Around midnight, your client allegedly broke into an empty stereo store, where she stole $2,000 worth of equipment. You have been asked to research the Kansas laws applicable to this situation. Table 1-3 provides examples of research terms you might use to begin work on this project.

In initial brainstorming, the goal is to produce as many terms as possible. But when you begin researching, you want to use those terms that appear on the list most often or that seem most important. As your research progresses, you will learn new research terms to include in the list and decide to take others off. For example, a secondary source may refer to a *term of art*, a word or phrase that has special meaning in a particular area of law. Later in your research, you may read cases that give you insights into the key words judges tend to use in discussing this topic. These terms and words need to be added to the list. You should also review the list periodically to help you refine your research. If an online search produces far too many results, review the list for more specific search terms. On the other hand, if the terms you use initially produce no hits, review the list for alternative, more general terms.

---

3. *See* Roy M. Mersky & Donald J. Dunn, *Fundamentals of Legal Research* 15 (8th ed., Found. Press 2002) (explaining "TARP," a similar mnemonic device).

Table 1-3. Generating Research Terms

Journalistic Approach

Who:	Thief, robber, burglar, business owner, property owner
What:	Burglary, aggravated burglary, crime, stolen goods
How:	Breaking and entering, trespassing
Why:	Theft, stealing
When:	Midnight
Where:	Empty store, building, commercial establishment, business, shop

TARPP Approach

Things:	Stolen goods
Actions:	Burglary, breaking and entering, trespassing, damages, crime
Remedies:	Burglary, aggravated burglary, incarceration
People:	Thief, robber, burglar, business owner, property owner
Places:	Empty store, building, commercial establishment, business, shop

B. Choosing to Research in Print or Online

Developing a comprehensive research strategy includes deciding when and how to best use print and online sources. Mark Herrmann, in a piece discussing what he calls "The Ten Most Common Mistaken Assumptions Made By New Lawyers," notes that "[m]ost new lawyers begin their legal research by turning on a computer. This is almost invariably wrong. When you work for me, do not begin your research with a computerized database unless I expressly tell you to do so."[4]

Herrmann discusses the inability of legal researchers searching primary law databases to map out the general outline of an area of law before they search for individual landmarks in that area. Accordingly, legal researchers should typically first use paper-based secondary sources such as treatises, then move on to case digests before reading

---

4. Mark Herrmann, *This Is What I'm Thinking: A Dialogue Between Partner and Associate ... From the Partner*, 25 Litigation 8 (1998).

cases. In other words, use the same sources researchers have been consulting for over a century.

Print materials, organized by topic, impart the cultural significance of learning how lawyers have traditionally thought about the law. Through no fault of their own, law students are just insufficiently knowledgeable on the law to be able to use online research as a first step.

1. Determining the Advantages of Print and Online Sources

With Hermann's admonition in mind, ask yourself the following questions in deciding whether to use print or online sources at each step of your research.

a. Where is the document available?

Recent primary authority is increasingly available both in print and online. Some important secondary sources may be available only in print, while some resources used to find and update the law are available only online. Do not assume that there is universal overlap between print and online sources.

b. How fast and how efficient will research be?

Many researchers find that *beginning* legal research in print is more productive than beginning online because books tend to provide more context, which keeps the project focused. In addition, most attorneys find it easier to read more carefully and thoroughly in print than on a computer screen. Online research has a number of advantages, though, including the ease of searching and the convenience of downloading or printing important documents.

c. What is the document?

Novice legal researchers sometimes find it difficult to distinguish between different types of documents online. In print sources, different types of authorities often appear in separate books, making it easy to tell them apart. In contrast, many documents look the same on a computer screen. Moreover, hyperlinks in online sources allow you to jump from a case to a statute to an article in a few clicks. In an actual library, those moves may take you to different shelves or even different floors. If you favor the tactility of print research, you may prefer researching in a law library instead of online sources.

d. Who wrote the document?

Be sure that you know who wrote a document before you base your analysis on it. Remember that only some documents are binding and authoritative. Documents written by courts, legislatures, and administrative agencies are "the law." Articles and treatises written by recognized experts in a field are not binding, but they can be very persuasive and are often authoritative. These types of documents are often available both in print and online. However, there are many other documents online, such as student-written comments and notes, with little or no authoritative value. Always consider how much weight a court will likely accord any given source.

e. How accurate is the document?

Print material tends to be more accurate than online versions of the same documents. The very process of publishing, with its numerous stages of editing and revising, ensures a high level of reliability. In contrast, online material is often valued for the speed with which it becomes available. With this speed comes an inevitable sacrifice of accuracy; even reputable services post documents with less editing than a book would warrant. If you need to quote an authority, or are otherwise relying on very precise language from it, print sources are always preferable.

f. When was the document published?

Print sources take longer to reach the researcher than online sources. To find the most current material, online sources often provide a clear advantage. But even websites may contain outdated material; you still need to determine whether an online document has a date indicating when it was posted or last updated. If no such date is available, at least note when you visited the website for reference later on.

When using an online database, you must also ensure that it covers a period of time relevant to your research. Online sources tend to cover more recent periods; thus, finding older material may require using print sources. A notable exception is HeinOnline, which makes available older law review articles that often are not included in other online sources.[5]

g. How much context is provided?

Most print sources include tables of contents or outlines that provide an overview of the legal area. These tools can provide context so that a novice researcher can understand the big picture before concentrating on a narrow legal issue. An increasing number of online sources also provide these tools, and when searching online you should use them whenever they are available. Clicking on a table of contents link can show where a document is placed within related material. This tactic is especially helpful when an online search lands you in the middle of a single document and you lack the visual clues or the context to understand how that document relates to the bigger picture.

Many lawyers—from novices to experts—have stories about the great case or article that they stumbled across while looking for something else. These stories result not just from serendipity, but from using resources that put related information together. In the library, scan the books shelved nearby helpful sources, and skim through relevant books to see whether other sections are on point. Sometimes online searching also produces serendipitous results; if you feel you may be close to the exact material you need but cannot find it, try using an online table of contents link to reorient yourself.

---

5. HeinOnline also offers comprehensive retrospective databases of other important resources, such as the *Federal Register* and *Statutes at Large*.

h. How much does it cost, and who is paying?

Some sources are free to use. Print sources are "free" in the sense that the library has already paid for them. Online sources provided by governments and universities are also free. When cost is an issue, consider using these sources first.

Online research using commercial services, on the other hand, can be very expensive. A single research project, poorly conceived and sloppily done, can cost hundreds or even thousands of dollars. But never assume online research is *too* expensive—its efficiency is often worth its price. Moreover, many law offices are finding that they can negotiate reasonable flat rates that allow them access to the narrow set of online sources they use routinely in their practice.

Check the billing practices in your office before using commercial online sources: What is your office's contract with the online provider? How will your office pass along charges to clients? How much are the clients willing to pay? Will the office cover the costs of online pro bono work? Also be sure you know your office's policy regarding the printing of online documents, which often brings extra charges.

2. Online Sources for Legal Research

The best way to find accurate and authoritative material online is by using highly regarded and dependable sites. The following are examples of established, reputable online research sites. For each site, look for a link such as "Help" or "Searching Hints" to provide information about finding material on that site. Some sites also offer online tutorials to introduce their resources and search processes.

a. Commercial Providers

LexisNexis and Westlaw are the largest commercial providers of computerized legal research. Both have reputations for accurate material and user-friendly search techniques.[6] They provide extensive

---

6. LexisNexis, however, has historically been less friendly to browsers other than Internet Explorer. If you are not using Internet Explorer, some of the features discussed in this book may not be available.

coverage of primary and secondary authority. Other commercial providers of legal materials include Loislaw and VersusLaw. They tend to be less expensive than LexisNexis and Westlaw, but they also provide less extensive coverage. Some of these providers allow you to search their sites as a visitor before deciding whether to subscribe to their services.

b. Government and University Websites

Government entities and universities generally provide access to their website information for free. These sites may contain less information than is available from the commercial providers, and the search engines on these sites tend to be more primitive. However, the amount of information available on these sites is increasing, making them more useful research tools. Given that they are free, they are almost always worth exploring.

Like other states, Kansas maintains its own websites for its primary authority. Although the print versions are the "official" authority, the online versions are useful for research. The primary limitation to these sites is that material may be available only for recent years. Some of the crucial websites for legal research in Kansas are:

- Kansas Government at www.kansas.gov/government
- Kansas Judicial Branch at www.kscourts.org
- Kansas Legislature at www.kslegislature.org
- Kansas Governor at www.governor.ks.gov
- Kansas Attorney General at www.ksag.org
- Kansas Secretary of State at www.kssos.org.

In addition, a number of universities maintain websites that provide reliable information. For Kansas material, the following links are helpful:

- University of Kansas Wheat Law Library
  at www.law.ku.edu/library
- Washburn University Law Library
  at www.washburnlaw.edu/library.

Other libraries contain links to valuable sites, even when the library itself does not maintain the material. Two examples are Cornell Law School's "Legal Information Institute" at www.law.cornell.edu and Washburn University School of Law's "WashLaw" at www.washlaw.edu. The Kansas segments of those websites list links to Kansas cases, statutes, administrative materials, and more. A similar "gateway" site is FindLaw at www.findlaw.com.

3. *Searching LexisNexis and Westlaw*

Each website has a different method for retrieving information, though all tend to follow similar algorithms. Because most websites are constantly being revised and because their search methods change over time, only general information is possible in an overview such as this. The following explanations are primarily for LexisNexis and Westlaw,[7] though much of the information should be easily applicable to other online sources.

a. *Beginning Research with a Citation*

When you have a citation to a case, statute, article, or other legal source, retrieving that document online is as simple as typing the citation into a designated box on the proper screen. In LexisNexis, click on "Get a Document" and type in the citation. (See Figure 1-4.) In Westlaw, type the citation into the "Find by citation" box that appears in the left frame. (See Figure 1-5.) Each service also allows you to retrieve cases by party name.

b. *Terms and Connectors Searching*

Both LexisNexis and Westlaw, as well as most search engines, allow you to conduct a search simply by typing in a single word. If the word is a term of art like "interpleader" or a cause of action that is less common, for example "kidnapping," this one-word

---

7. In addition, LexisNexis and Westlaw provide ample training material in print and on their websites. For research assistance, call LexisNexis at (800) 455-3947 and Westlaw at (800) 733-2889.

Figure 1-4. "Get a Document" on LexisNexis

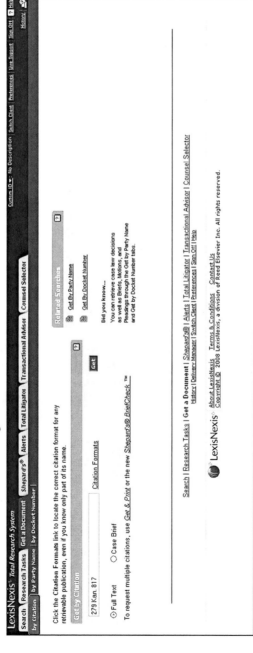

Source: LexisNexis. Copyright 2008 LexisNexis, a division of Reed Elsevier Inc. All Rights Reserved. LexisNexis and the Knowledge Burst logo are registered trademarks of Reed Elsevier Properties Inc. and are used with the permission of LexisNexis.

Figure 1-5. "Find by citation" on Westlaw

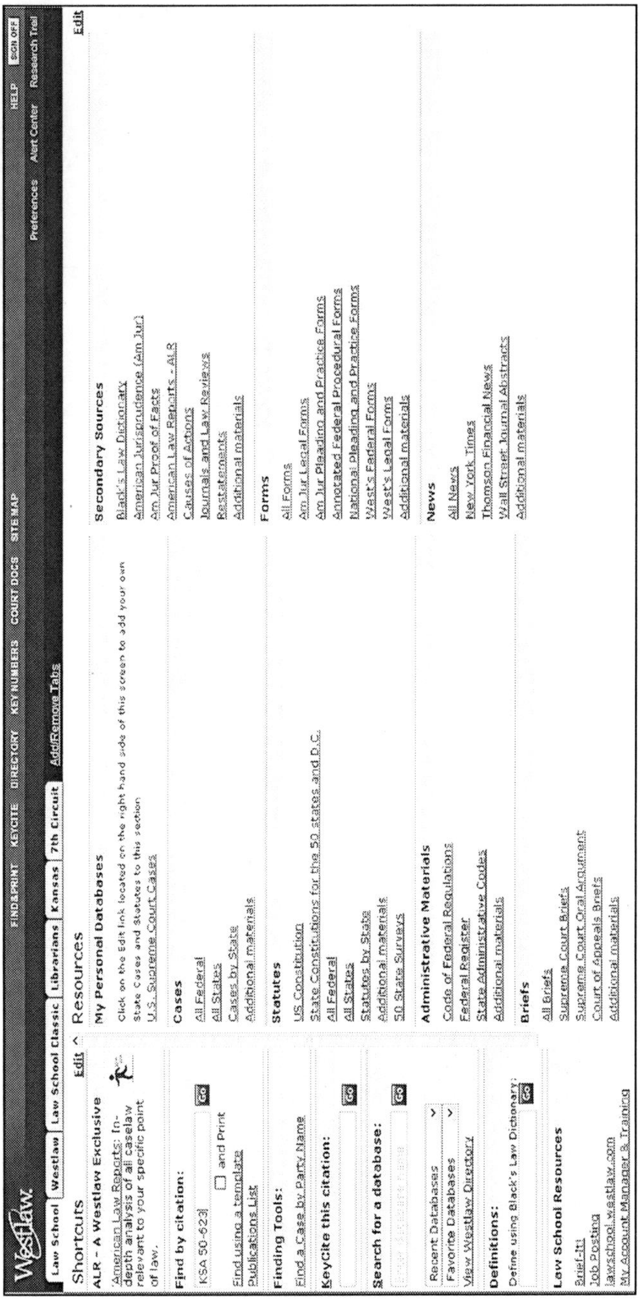

Westlaw.

FIND&PRINT　KEYCITE　DIRECTORY　KEYNUMBERS　COURT DOCS　SITE MAP　　Preferences　Alert Center　Research Trail　HELP　SIGN OFF

Law School | Westlaw | Law School Classic | Librarians | Kansas | 7th Circuit | Add/Remove Tabs

Shortcuts　Edit ^

ALR - A Westlaw Exclusive
American Law Reports: In-depth analysis of all caselaw relevant to your specific point of law.

Find by citation:
KSA 50-623|　Go
☐ and Print
Find using a template
Publications List

Finding Tools:
Find a Case by Party Name

KeyCite this citation:
　Go

Search for a database:
　Go

Recent Databases ＞
Favorite Databases ＞
View Westlaw Directory

Definitions:
Define using Black's Law Dictionary:
　Go

Law School Resources
Brief It!
Job Posting
lawschool.westlaw.com
My Account Manager & Training

Resources　Edit ^

My Personal Databases
Click on the Edit link located on the right hand side of this screen to add your own State Cases and Statutes to this section
U.S. Supreme Court Cases

Cases
All Federal
All States
Cases by State
Additional materials

Statutes
US Constitution
State Constitutions for the 50 states and D.C.
All Federal
All States
Statutes by State
Additional materials
50 State Surveys

Administrative Materials
Code of Federal Regulations
Federal Register
State Administrative Codes
Additional materials

Briefs
All Briefs
Supreme Court Briefs
Supreme Court Oral Argument
Court of Appeals Briefs
Additional materials

Secondary Sources
Black's Law Dictionary
American Jurisprudence (Am Jur)
Am Jur Proof of Facts
American Law Reports - ALR
Causes of Actions
Journals and Law Reviews
Restatements
Additional materials

Forms
All Forms
Am Jur Legal Forms
Am Jur Pleading and Practice Forms
Annotated Federal Procedural Forms
National Pleading and Practice Forms
West's Federal Forms
West's Legal Forms
Additional materials

News
All News
New York Times
Thomson Financial News
Wall Street Journal Abstracts
Additional materials

Source: Westlaw. Reprinted with permission of Thomson Reuters/West.

search may be very successful. In contrast, if the search is for a broad area like "murder" or "jurisdiction," you will need to add more terms.

You can create more specific searches using Boolean connectors.[8] These connectors tell the computer how terms should be placed in relation to one another in targeted documents, enabling you to more accurately control what the computer searches for. To use terms and connectors searching effectively, think of the ideal document you would like to find and try to imagine where your search terms would be located in relation to each other within that document. Would they be in the same sentence? The same paragraph? A sample search in a question of the enforceability of a covenant not to compete is: *covenant /s compete.* Table 1-6 summarizes the most common connectors and commands. Chapter 11 explains terms and connectors searching in more detail.

c. Natural Language Searching

LexisNexis and Westlaw allow natural language searching, which may be most similar to online searching in non-legal contexts. Simply type in a question or sentence and let the computer program decide which words are critical, whether the words should appear in some proximity to one another, and how often they appear in the document. In the previous example, the following sentence could be used as a natural language search: *Is a covenant not to compete enforceable against a former employee?* (See Figure 1-7.) While natural language searching is unlikely to produce an exhaustive list of relevant authorities, it may result in a few relevant cases that could spark other research. For this reason, some researchers like to conduct a natural language search early in their research.

---

8. George Boole was a British mathematician. The Boolean connectors that carry his name dictate the logical relationship of search terms to each other.

Table 1-6. Boolean Connectors and Commands

Goal	LexisNexis	Westlaw
To find alternative terms anywhere in the document	or blank space	or
To find both terms anywhere in the document	and &	and &
To find both terms within a particular distance from each other	/p = in 1 paragraph /s = in 1 sentence /n = within *n* words	/p = in 1 paragraph /s = in 1 sentence /n = within *n* words
To find terms used as a phrase	leave a blank space between each word of the phrase	put the phrase in quotation marks
To control the hierarchy of searching	parentheses	parentheses
To exclude terms	and not	but not %
To extend the end of a term	!	!
To hold the place of letters in a term	*	*

d. Table of Contents Searching

Online providers sometimes provide access to a table of contents for a particular database; this works just like a table of contents in print. For example, in a dispute over whether an injury that occurred at work is covered by Kansas's workers' compensation laws, you could open the table of contents for Kansas statutes and scan the list of chapters until you found "Labor and Industries." Clicking on that link would open the list of articles under

Figure 1-7. Natural Language Search on LexisNexis

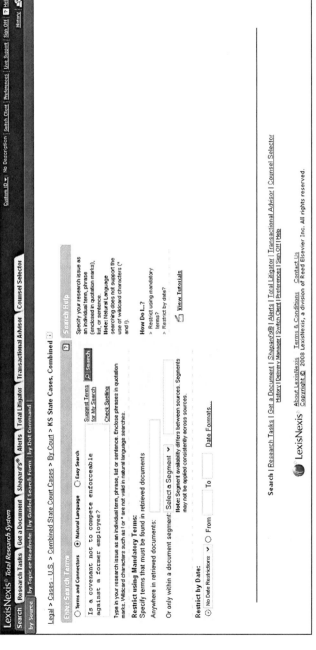

Figure 1-8. Table of Contents Searching on Westlaw

Source: Westlaw. Reprinted with permission of Thomson Reuters/West.

that chapter, including Article 5 on "Workers Compensation." Another click would provide a list of the statutes in that article. (See Figure 1-8.)

e. Topic Searching

Both LexisNexis and Westlaw have tools for topic searching. The most user-friendly of these tools allow the researcher to begin with a list of broad areas of law and narrow the topic by clicking through successive lists. On LexisNexis this tool was previously called "Search Advisor," but can now be found under "Search by Topic or Headnote"; on Westlaw it is "KeySearch." As an example, to find cases on whether an injury resulting from a fight in the workplace is compensable under Kansas's workers' compensation laws, you might begin on LexisNexis by clicking on "Search by Topic or Headnote" and selecting "Workers' Compensation & SSDI," in the broad list, then selecting successively "Compensability" and, after expanding the list with the "plus" symbol, "Injuries." Once you have narrowed the topic sufficiently and selected a jurisdiction, the computer will retrieve cases on point. The same process applies to Westlaw, although the precise terminology will vary. As with natural language searching, topic searching may be useful as a starting point, but it is unlikely to produce a comprehensive list of authorities.

f. Databases and Kansas Tabs

Before searching either with terms and connectors or with natural language, you need to select a database (also called a "source") in which to run your search. To find a database on LexisNexis, go to the "Search" tab and review the list of sources. Clicking on "View more sources" will reveal additional databases. On Westlaw, a complete list of databases is available from the "Directory" link at the top of every screen.

Both services have compiled Kansas databases under a tab that you can add to the default set of search tabs. On LexisNexis, use the "Research System" and the "Search" tabs, and then click on "Add/Edit Tabs." Westlaw allows you to do the same from any page by clicking "Add/Remove Tabs."

Note that on Westlaw, the tabbed screen does not provide information about the contents of each database. That information is available through the Westlaw "Directory," in which each database listed is followed by an "i" in a grey circle. LexisNexis provides this information on its sources through an "i" link as well. Before using any database for the first time, check the "i" information icon to learn what documents are contained and the dates of coverage.

V. Researching the Law—Organization of This Book

The remainder of this book explains how to conduct legal research in a variety of sources. Chapter 2 addresses the Kansas Constitution, which is the highest legal authority in the state. Because the research process often begins with a search for background and context, the book examines secondary sources in Chapter 3. Chapters 4 and 5 explain how to research judicial decisions. Chapter 6 explains how to update legal authority using KeyCite and Shepard's. Chapters 7 and 8 describe statutory and legislative history research, respectively. Chapter 9 addresses administrative law.

Chapter 10 offers guidance for the specialized task of researching legal ethics. Although each chapter includes relevant website addresses for online research, Chapter 11 provides additional information for conducting legal research online. Chapter 12 discusses research strategies as well as how to organize your research. You may prefer to skim that chapter now and refer to it frequently, even though a number of references in it will not become clear until you have read the intervening chapters.

Appendix A provides an overview of the conventions lawyers follow in citing legal authority in their documents. Appendix B contains a selected bibliography of texts on legal research and analysis. The general research texts tend to concentrate on federal resources, supplementing this book's brief introduction to those resources.

Chapter 2

The Kansas Constitution

The Kansas Constitution establishes and defines the organization of the state's government. A constitution is the written instrument agreed upon by the people of a state as the absolute rule of action and decision for all departments and officers in respect to all the points covered by it. It must control until changed by the authority that established it (i.e., by amendment).

The Wyandotte Convention, which drafted the Constitution of the State of Kansas, met between the 5th and the 29th of July in 1859. Of the 52 delegates, 18 were lawyers, 16 were farmers, 8 were merchants, and the remainder included doctors, surveyors, mechanics, and printers. The Wyandotte Convention was the fourth constitutional convention in Kansas in less than four years—and the first in which both political parties were represented. The other three conventions had been marked by fraud, force, or intervention by the federal government. The Wyandotte delegates used the constitution of an older state as a model, choosing the Ohio Constitution by vote.

The Kansas Constitution was adopted at Wyandotte on July 29, 1859, as amended. It was ratified on October 4, 1859, by a vote of 10,421 to 5,530. In the Ordinance of the Kansas Constitution, the U.S. Congress agreed to conditions concerning school sections, university lands, lands for public buildings, lands for benevolent institutions, salt springs, and mines.

Table 2-1. Articles of the Kansas Constitution

Article 1	Executive
Article 2	Legislative
Article 3	Judicial
Article 4	Elections
Article 5	Suffrage
Article 6	Education
Article 7	Public Institutions and Welfare
Article 8	Militia
Article 9	County and Township Organization
Article 10	Apportionment of the Legislature
Article 11	Finance and Taxation
Article 12	Corporations
Article 13	Banks
Article 14	Constitutional Amendment and Revision
Article 15	Miscellaneous

I. Researching the Kansas Constitution

The Kansas Constitution itself is divided into articles, which are subdivided into sections. For example, Article 1 concerns the executive branch. Article 1, Section 3 vests executive power in the governor; Article 1, Section 7 specifically gives the governor pardoning power. The Kansas Bill of Rights is divided into sections. Many of these rights mirror those in the federal constitution, including the right to free speech and the right to bear arms. The articles of the Kansas Constitution are listed in Table 2-1, and the sections of the Kansas Bill of Rights are listed in Table 2-2.

Table 2-2. Sections of the Kansas Bill of Rights

§ 1. Equal rights.
§ 2. Political power; privileges.
§ 3. Right of peaceable assembly; petition.
§ 4. Bear arms; armies.
§ 5. Trial by jury.
§ 6. Slavery prohibited.
§ 7. Religious liberty.
§ 8. Habeas corpus.
§ 9. Bail.
§ 10. Trial; defense of accused.
§ 11. Liberty of press and speech; libel.
§ 12. No forfeiture of estate for crimes.
§ 13. Treason.
§ 14. Soldiers' quarters.
§ 15. Search and seizure.
§ 16. Imprisonment for debt.
§ 17. Property rights of citizens and aliens.
§ 18. Justice without delay.
§ 19. Emoluments or privileges prohibited.
§ 20. Powers retained by people.

A. The Constitution in *Kansas Statutes Annotated*

The principal source of constitutional material in Kansas is the constitution volume of *Kansas Statutes Annotated* (KSA), which contains the following:

- Organic Act: An Act to Organize the Territory of Kansas (1854)
- Act for Admission of Kansas into Union (1861)
- Constitution of the State of Kansas, including the Kansas Bill of Rights
- Subject lists, amendments and proposed amendments to the Kansas Constitution
- The Declaration of Independence
- Constitution of the United States
- Comparative table of sections.

There is no index to the Kansas Constitution in the constitution volume. Instead, search the *General Index to the Kansas Statutes Annotated*, located at the end of the KSA volumes. Index entries to the Kansas Constitution are found under the boldface heading CONSTITUTION OF KANSAS in the *General Index to the Kansas Statutes Annotated*.

With the article and section of a relevant provision of the Kansas Constitution, or with the section number of a relevant provision in the Kansas Bill of Rights, turn to the relevant language in the constitution volume.

After each article or section of the Kansas Constitution, a list called *Research and Practice Aids* includes references to West's key-number digest system.[1] References are also made to the legal encyclopedias, *American Jurisprudence 2d* and *Corpus Juris Secundum*, and current forms and practice books applicable to Kansas, most of which are published by Thomson/West.[2]

Next, *Law Reviews and Bar Journal References* contains citations to the *Journal of the Kansas Bar Association, University of Kansas Law Review, Washburn Law Journal, Journal of the Kansas Trial Lawyer Association*, and *Kansas Journal of Law and Public Policy*. Any pertinent Kansas attorney general opinions are also cited.

After *Research and Practice Aids, Law Reviews and Bar Journal References*, and other authorities that discuss particular sections or articles, there are short case annotations listed giving a short summary of each relevant case. Citations to the full cases accompany the annotations. Do not rely on the short summary; reading the text of the source itself will allow you to analyze its relevance to your research.

A soft-cover pamphlet to KSA comes out once a year, updating information in the bound volumes.

---

1. Digests are explained in Chapter 5.
2. These secondary sources are covered in Chapter 3.

B. Free Online Sources of the Kansas Constitution

The full text of the constitution is available on the State Library of Kansas Information Desk website at www.kslib.info/constitution/. This site also contains the Kansas ordinance and the preamble to the constitution along with the Kansas Bill of Rights.

C. The Kansas Constitution on LexisNexis and Westlaw

LexisNexis and Westlaw provide the Kansas Constitution and extensive annotations under their Kansas tabs. From the Kansas tab on LexisNexis, you might need to click "View more sources" to find a database containing just the constitution (as opposed to a combined database containing the constitution, statutes, and other authority). On Westlaw, the Kansas Constitution is included in the statutory databases, KS-ST and KS-ST-ANN. To search just the constitution, you can go through the table of contents for either database. Alternatively, you can search an entire statutory database using as one of your search terms "pr (*Constitution of Kansas*)," which will retrieve only documents having "Constitution of Kansas" in the preliminary field.

II. Interpreting the Kansas Constitution

The primary duty of the Kansas courts in interpreting the Kansas Constitution is to look at the intention of the drafters (the legislature) and the adopters (the voters) of the provision.[3]

A constitutional provision is not to be narrowly or technically construed, but its language should be interpreted to mean what the words

---

3. *State ex. rel. Stephan v. Finney*, 254 Kan. 632, 654 (1994).

Table 2-3. Comparison of Constitutional Wording
Regarding Cruel and Unusual Punishment

Kansas Constitution
§ 9 of the Bill of Rights

All persons shall be bailable by sufficient sureties except for capital offenses, where proof is evident or the presumption great. Excessive bail shall not be required, nor excessive fines imposed, nor cruel **or** unusual punishment inflicted.

United States Constitution
Eighth Amendment

Excessive bail shall not be required, nor excessive fines imposed, nor cruel **and** unusual punishments inflicted.

Note: Emphasis added.

imply to persons of common understanding.[4] Words in common usage are to be given their natural and ordinary meaning in arriving at a proper construction.[5]

A. Text and Case Law

Begin by reading the words of the constitutional provision carefully. If it is a lengthy provision, outlining it may help. Then read cases that address that provision. Also, reading the cases cited in those cases may provide important context.

Do not assume that cases interpreting the federal constitution also interpret Kansas's constitution. For example, Section 9 of the Kansas Bill of Rights is textually distinguishable from the Eighth Amendment of the federal constitution. (See Table 2-3.) Section 9 departs from the language of the Eighth Amendment, forbidding "cruel or unusual punishments" as opposed to "cruel and unusual

---

4. *Colorado Interstate Gas Co. v. Bd. of Morton County Commoners*, 247 Kan. 654, 660 (1990).

5. *Farmers Co-op v. Kansas Bd. of Tax Appeals*, 236 Kan. 632, 635 (1985).

punishments." Several states have found this difference of language significant; Kansas, however, has not. In *State v. Scott*, the Kansas Supreme Court stated there is no substantial difference between the two provisions.[6]

B. Historical Context

To interpret the state constitution, Kansas courts will also look at the historical context in which an article or an amendment to an article was created. For example, since 1861 Kansas has broadly prohibited lotteries.[7] The term "lottery" has been defined by the Kansas courts over the years to mean any game, scheme, gift, enterprise, or similar contrivance in which persons agree to give valuable consideration for a chance to win a prize or prizes.[8]

In 1974, however, the Kansas voters amended Article 15 § 3 of the constitution to permit bingo games to be conducted by bona fide nonprofit religious, charitable and fraternal, educational, and veterans organizations.[9] In 1986, Kansas voters amended the constitution to permit pari-mutuel wagering in horse and dog racing.[10] On November 4, 1986, Kansas citizens amended the Kansas Constitution to authorize a state-owned and state-operated lottery.[11]

In upholding the 1986 amendment, the Kansas Supreme Court looked at the historical context and stated that, between 1833 and 1860, lotteries were abolished in all but three states. It was not surprising, then, that Kansas saw fit at the time to prohibit lotteries. The high court stated that the intent of the voters in approving the lottery

---

6. "Although we have the right to interpret our Kansas Constitution in a manner different than the United States Constitution has been construed, we have not traditionally done so. The wording of both clauses at issue is nearly identical, and we look to constructions of both provisions in reaching our conclusions herein." *State v. Scott*, 265 Kan. 1, 5 (1998).

7. Kan. Const. art. 15, § 3 (1861).

8. *State ex rel. Stephan v. Finney*, 251 Kan. 559, 569 (1992).

9. Kan. Const. art. 15, § 3a (1974).

10. Kan. Const. art. 15, § 3b (1986).

11. *State ex rel. Stephan v. Finney*, 254 Kan. 632, 634 (1994).

in 1986, however, was to allow closely regulated gambling and to raise money for the state. A multistate lottery, therefore, would not be repugnant to the state.[12]

C. Constitutional Amendment and Revision

A constitutional amendment requires the approval of two-thirds of each house of the legislature and a majority of actual votes cast by citizens on the amendment. Not more than five amendments can be submitted at the same election. There is no constitutional amendment procedure by initiative in Kansas.

The call for a constitutional convention also requires the approval of two-thirds of each house of the legislature and a majority of actual votes cast on the proposal by the people. The periodic submission of the convention question to the people about whether to hold a constitutional convention is not required.[13]

A list of amendments and proposed amendments to the Kansas Constitution follows the Kansas Constitution in KSA. Of the 123 amendments proposed between 1861 and 2007, 92 have passed. Those that have passed are interspersed throughout the constitution—not in a separate section at the end. For example, in 1972 a proposition to repeal Section 5 of Article 5 relating to duelists passed although the other sections failed.

III. Researching the United States Constitution

The United States Constitution is published in the constitution volume of the KSA. Entries are found under the boldface heading CONSTITUTION OF THE UNITED STATES in the *General Index to the Kansas Statutes Annotated*. Remember to update constitution print

---

12. *Id.* at 650.
13. Kan. Const. art. 14.

research by looking to the KSA pamphlet supplement, which comes out once a year.

The United States Constitution is also available in print in the first volumes of *United States Code Annotated* and *United States Code Service*. Although these series are primarily used to research federal statutes, the publishers include the United States Constitution as a convenience for readers. These series are explained in Chapter 7. Additionally, publications of other states' codes may include the United States Constitution, just as the KSA does.

The United States Constitution is also available online at both state and federal websites. Some addresses of relevant sites include:

· www.findlaw.com/casecode/constitution, which features a keyword search function and hyperlinks to articles, amendments, and annotations
· www.archives.gov, which provides the original text with hyperlinks to amendments
· www.law.emory.edu/FEDERAL/usconst.html, a university site that provides a search engine.

In addition, the United States Constitution is available on Lexis-Nexis and Westlaw. Follow the suggestions above regarding the Kansas Constitution to locate and search databases containing the federal constitution.

Chapter 3

Secondary Sources

Secondary sources provide an overview of the law. The sources may synthesize and explain difficult rules and principles surrounding the legal issues being researched. The secondary sources may provide a framework for interpreting the specific facts of a research problem. It is usually wise to start a legal research query with a secondary source, especially if you have little or no background regarding the legal issue being researched. You can save yourself a lot of time by using secondary sources to take advantage of all the research and analysis someone else has already done.

In addition, secondary sources may direct you to relevant primary authorities. Although secondary sources by definition are non-binding on a court, the primary authorities in the footnotes can often lead to cases, statutes, or regulations that are mandatory or persuasive authority in the relevant jurisdiction.

I. Legal Encyclopedias

Legal encyclopedias are very similar in concept and organization to general encyclopedias. Just like general encyclopedias, legal encyclopedias are written in narrative form and arranged alphabetically by subject, in this case by legal subject. Legal encyclopedias are introductory. They are not evaluative or analytical. They give an expository introduction to the propositions of law surrounding almost all legal subjects. Some states have encyclopedias for their law, but Kansas does not. The two national encyclopedias are *American Jurisprudence 2d (Am Jur 2d)* and *Corpus Juris Secundum (CJS)*.

A. *American Jurisprudence 2d (Am Jur 2d)*

Am Jur 2d is arranged alphabetically under more than 400 legal topics. Some lawyers and even educators state that *Am Jur 2d*, now published by Thomson/West, and its counterpart, *Corpus Juris Secundum (CJS)*, are fungible. Don't be fooled. Until recently, *Am Jur 2d* was published by Lawyers Cooperative Publishing. The editorial approach Lawyers Cooperative Publishing took was distinct from the West publishing notion of total recall, giving the lawyers every single case. Lawyers Coop used more editorial enhancement, providing lawyers what they thought to be the more important cases. Even though *Am Jur 2d* is now published by Thomson/West, this distinction between *Am Jur 2d* and *CJS* has been maintained to a large degree.

Am Jur 2d has a multi-volume general index where you can find a relevant topic. It also has a Table of Statutes volume for finding a relevant topic discussing a particular section of the U.S. Code, a federal court rule, a regulation, or a uniform law. After locating the right volume containing your topic, check the volume index to find the relevant sections within the topic. Make certain you consult the pocket part under the same topic, sections, and footnotes you found useful. Another feature that makes *Am Jur 2d* distinct is the New Topic Section volume, which covers newer topics that have not yet been incorporated into the larger set. You will find this volume at the end of the entire set. It is one of the "just in case" research tools you should check.

B. *Corpus Juris Secundum (CJS)*

CJS is the second series of the first legal encyclopedia published, *Corpus Juris*. Created with the West philosophy of giving lawyers every case and letting them decide which cases are important, *CJS* is so heavily footnoted with case law that some pages may only contain a small blurb of text while the rest of the page is filled with case footnotes.

Am Jur 2d, known for its Table of Statutes volume, has led West Publishing to include a Table of Statutes and Regulations section in newer, recompiled volumes of *CJS*. *CJS* also has a section in front of each topic called "Analysis," which breaks down the title into roman numerals and alphabetical letters. The outline helps the researcher eliminate larger sections of inapplicable material and narrow the search to relevant information. As when researching with *Am Jur 2d*, you should first check the *CJS* general index to find a relevant title. Next, check the volume index for the most precise sections within the title. Always check the volume pocket part under the same relevant title, section, and footnotes to ensure you have the most recent information.

C. Using Legal Encyclopedias

Both encyclopedias have good cross-reference schemes. Older volumes of *CJS* cross-reference the topic and key numbers of the West digest system. Newer volumes of *CJS* cross-reference to both the West digest system and *American Law Reports*. Older volumes of *Am Jur 2d* cross-reference *American Law Reports*. Newer volumes of *Am Jur 2d* cross-reference both *American Law Reports* and the West digest system.

Unfortunately, legal encyclopedias' utility as a secondary source has been abused by various attorneys and courts.[1] This holds true in the state of Kansas where the most cited secondary source is *Am Jur 2d*.[2] Over a fifteen-year period from 1982 through 1996, the Kansas Supreme Court cited *Am Jur 2d* 242 times as the "sole authority" supporting a point of law, while the Kansas Court of Appeals did the same 186 times. It is improper to cite a legal encyclopedia as a sole and final authority on any point of law because the immediate case at bar may be distinct in law or fact from the many footnoted cases supporting the general narrative in the encyclopedia.

---

1. *See* Mersky & Dunn, *Fundamentals of Legal Research* 350 (8th ed., Found. Press 2002).

2. Joseph Custer, *Citation Practices of the Kansas Supreme Court and Kansas Court of Appeals*, 8 Kan J.L. & Pub. Policy 126, 131 (1999).

This is not a criticism of legal encyclopedias, but only a commentary on how they have been misused by lawyers and courts from time to time. They remain excellent indexes and introductory guides to the law. They are valuable publications to be consulted at the early stages of legal research. Encyclopedias are a good source for cross-referencing other useful secondary sources on topic (see Figure 3-1).

To use an encyclopedia online, you can either do a terms and connectors search or browse the encyclopedia's table of contents. The table of contents for both national encyclopedias is long and detailed, so you may need to look under several topics before you find a section on point. On Westlaw, both *Am Jur 2d* and *CJS* are listed under "Treatises, CLEs, Practice Guides" in the directory. On LexisNexis, *Am Jur 2d* is available under "Secondary Legal-Jurisprudences & Encyclopedias" in the directory. *CJS* is not available on LexisNexis.

II. *American Law Reports* (*ALR*)

ALR is an annotated case reporter with indexes and supplements. Federal materials were put in a series of their own in 1969, called the *American Law Reports Federal* (*ALR Fed*). *ALR* usually selects cases from throughout the country with specific facts often focusing on a developing or controversial legal issue.

Until *ALR 5th*, an annotation followed each opinion. The annotation is a legal essay on the point of law illustrated by a selected case, giving the background and issues involved, and summarizing the rules in all jurisdictions with decisions on point. The annotation cites these decisions and arranges them by jurisdiction. Among the thousands of annotations in the various series of *ALR*, there is a good chance of finding one on the point of law you are researching. In fact, *ALR* has become a legal research set driven by its annotations. Knowing that the re-publication of reported cases is secondary to the annotations, starting with *ALR 5th*, the publisher put the cases in the back of the volumes, after all the annotations. Also with *ALR 5th*, the

Figure 3-1. *American Jurisprudence 2d* Excerpt

§ 16	18 Am Jur 2d

§ 16 Derivative works

Research References

West's Key Number Digest, Copyright and Intellectual Property ⬯31
What Constitutes Derivative Work Under the Copyright Act of 1976, 149 A.L.R. Fed. 527
Copyright law—Derivative works—Seventh Circuit holds that mounting copyrighted notecards on ceramic tiles does not constitute preparation of derivative works in violation of the Copyright Act [Lee v. A.R.T. Co., 125 F.3d 580 (7th Cir. 1997)], 111 Harv LR 1365 (1999)

Publication of a derivative work constitutes publication of preexisting works contained therein.[1] In general, however, publication of a derivative work does not affect the validity of a copyright in a preexisting work, despite incorporation of the underlying work into the derivative work.[2]

◆ **Observation:** The Copyright Act of 1976 provides that in a case of derivative works incorporating previously published material, the year date of first publication of the compilation or derivative work in the copyright notice of the derivative work is sufficient to satisfy a notice requirement with respect to the underlying work.[3]

II. SUBJECT MATTER

A. COPYRIGHTABILITY, IN GENERAL

Statutory References
U.S. Const. Art I § 8 cl 8
17 U.S.C.A. §§ 101, 102; 301
18 U.S.C.A. §§ 1461, 1462, 1465

Research References

West's Digest References
Copyright and Intellectual Property ⬯4 to 10.4, 17

Annotation References
A.L.R. Digest: Copyright § 2
A.L.R. Index: Copyright and Literary Property

Forms References
Am. Jur. Legal Forms 2d, Copyright and Literary and Artistic Property § 72:191
Am. Jur. Pleading and Practice Forms, Copyright and Literary Property §§ 56, 78

Trial Strategy References
Copyright Infringement of Literary Works Including Compilations and Other Fact-Based Works, 20 Am. Jur. Proof of Facts 3d 431
Copyright Infringement Litigation, 77 Am. Jur. Trials 449

[Section 16]
[1]Harris Custom Builders, Inc. v. Hoffmeyer, 92 F.3d 517 (7th Cir. 1996).
[2]Harris Custom Builders, Inc. v. Hoffmeyer, 92 F.3d 517 (7th Cir. 1996).
Copyright in a preexisting work which is incorporated into a derivative work is not abrogated by publication of the new work. Stewart v. Abend, 495 U.S. 207, 110 S. Ct. 1750, 109 L. Ed. 2d 184 (1990).
[3]17 U.S.C.A. § 401(b)(2).

Source: *American Jurisprudence 2d*, volume 18, page 362 (2004). Reprinted with permission of Thomson Reuters/West.

publisher added West key numbers and computer-assisted legal research queries for the researcher.

This aspect should not, however, be a great concern because researchers rarely cite *ALR* annotations. The standard of writing in *ALR* is uneven over the series. An example of the substantive text of an annotation is given in Figure 3-2.

ALR has multiple indexes and supplements. The condensed softcover *Quick Index* (which indexes annotations from *ALR 3d* to present) includes both specific word entries and analytical entries. The six-volume *ALR Index to Annotations* covers all the *ALR* series except for *ALR 1st*, which has its own index. *ALR 3d, ALR 4th, ALR 5th, ALR 6th, ALR Fed,* and *ALR Fed 2d,* are supplemented by pocket parts. Other legal sources, such as *Am Jur 2d* and *Shepard's Case Citators* cross-reference *ALR* annotations. There are also two separate *ALR* digests. One digest is for *ALR 1st* and *ALR 2d.* Another is for *ALR 3d, ALR 4th, ALR 5th, ALR 6th, ALR Fed,* and *ALR Fed 2d.* The digest offers researchers the alternative to finding annotations via the analytical approach.

Although *ALR* is not strictly a Kansas legal research tool (rather, it is national in scope), it is widely relied on by Kansas attorneys. Practitioners in small towns in Kansas, who might have few legal research sets, will usually have *ALR* or electronic access to it. Discovering Kansas cases via *ALR* is quick and easy since cases are arranged by jurisdiction in the *Table of Jurisdictions*.

To search in *ALR*, go to the one-volume *Quick Index* to *ALR*. If what you are looking for is not in the *Quick Index*, go to the multi-volume *Index to Annotations*. After finding relevant topics, check the *Annotation History Table* at the back of the last volume of the *Index to Annotations* and its pocket part for supplementing or superseded annotations. If you find a supplementing annotation, use both the original annotation and supplementing annotation in your research. If you find a superseding annotation, use only that in your research. When reading the relevant annotation, check the *Analysis* and *Table of Jurisdictions* to find pertinent sections. Check § 1(b) "Related Matters" to find cites to other relevant annotations and newer law review articles. Remember to check the pocket part under the same annotation and annotation sections.

Figure 3-2. *ALR* Annotation Excerpt

§ 2[a]	"PIT BULL" REGULATION	80 ALR4th

80 ALR4th 70

question is itself fatal to a vagueness challenge.

In addition to challenges under the United States Constitution or the constitutions of the particular states, at least one ordinance specifically regulating the keeping and handling of dogs of the "Pit Bull" type has been successfully challenged because its subject matter was held to have been pre-empted by the state criminal code (§ 16).

[b] Practice pointers

Counsel for a dog owner, in attacking a "Pit Bull" statute or ordinance on vagueness grounds, will wish to emphasize to the greatest extent practicable the inherent confusion in identification of the particular allegedly dangerous breed among several breeds similar in appearance or name or both, but of which some are recognized by authorities to be relatively harmless.[3] This problem is accentuated by a statute or ordinance which does not, of its own terms, provide a reference source for determining the particular characteristics of the breed or set of breeds contemplated.[4] Facing this latter type of legislation, counsel should be able to make a strong case for unconstitutional vagueness based on the difficulties experienced by dog officers or other public officials concerned with the enforcement or

interpretation of such legislation to make an accurate identification of the target breed based on an unguided research of general descriptive reference sources.[5]

II. Police Power as Basis for Regulation

§ 3. Generally

A number of cases, including the following cases involving constitutional challenges to the validity of statutes or ordinances expressly governing "Pit Bull" dogs or the like, have held that the control of dogs is a matter within the legitimate exercise of the police power of a state or its subdivisions.

Upholding the constitutionality of a "Pit Bull" ordinance as a legitimate exercise of municipal police power, the court in Hearn v Overland Park (1989) 244 Kan 638, 772 P2d 758, 80 ALR4th 51, cert den (US) 107 L Ed 2d 503, 110 S Ct 500, declared that the police power is wide in scope and gives the governmental body broad powers to enact laws to promote the health, morals, and similarly valuable standards and conditions of the people. The court said that this power may be exerted as a restraint on private rights of persons or to regulate the use of property, and where appropriate or necessary, prohibit the use of property

---

3. See "The New Breed of Municipal Dog Control Laws: Are They Constitutional?," 53 University of Cincinnati Law Review 1067, at 1078-1080 (1984).

4. Compare State v Peters (1988, Fla App D3) 534 So 2d 760, 13 FLW 2517, review den (Fla) 542 So 2d 1334, involving such objective refer-

ence source citations, with Lima v McFadden (1986, Ohio App, Allen Co) Docket No. 1-85-22 (LEXIS® Slip Opinion), involving an ordinance with no internal reference to outside sources for identification.

5. American Dog Owners Asso. v Lynn (1989) 404 Mass 73, 533 NE2d 642.

Source: *American Law Reports 4th*, 80 ALR 4th 70, page 76 (1990). Reprinted with permission of Thomson Reuters/West.

III. *Restatements*

A. Background of *Restatements*

The *Restatements of the Law*, published by the American Law Institute (ALI), were an attempt in the early twentieth century to stem the ever-increasing flow of case law that was being unleashed by the West Publishing Company. One of the main ideas behind the creation of the *Restatements* was that no one should have to go to the voluminous cases again since the *Restatements* would cap off the law. There would be no cites to actual cases. Instead of named parties, like Smith versus Jones, the *Restatements* would refer to A versus B.

Despite the popularity of *Restatements*, the grand idea did not work. Even with the wonderful work of such scholars as Samuel Williston (*Restatement of Contracts*) and Richard Powell (*Restatement of Property*) available, the lawyers and courts still insisted on citing other sources of law to support their point. Over time, ALI allowed drafters the opportunity, during the composition period, to predict what the law would be. Thus, *Restatements* are no longer just a cap on what the law is, but also a predictor of what the law will or should be.

The *Restatements* were cited faithfully by both the Kansas Supreme Court and Kansas Court of Appeals from the period of 1982 through 1996.[3] In fact, the *Restatement of Torts* holds the distinction of being the second-most-cited secondary source after *American Jurisprudence 2d* in Kansas.[4] Even so, you should never rely solely on the *Restatement* to provide a statement of the law in Kansas. The *Restatement* may be more or less progressive than the law in Kansas. Keep in mind that *Restatements* typically offer more than one rule of law. Kansas may or may not have adopted all the particular rules regarding a specific point of law.

Restatements are not updated, even though most are published in both a first and a second series.[5] Some are now in a third. A later series does not necessarily supersede a specific rule in an earlier series.

---

3. Custer, *supra* n. 2, at 130–31.
4. *Id.* at 131.
5. The exceptions are the *Restatement of Restitution* and *Restatement of Security*.

If a court in your state has adopted a certain *Restatement* section, it will continue to be the law even if a subsequent version of the *Restatement* omits or alters its statement of the rule. Therefore, you may still need to research the first series of a *Restatement* in order to interpret a case that has adopted a section from that *Restatement*. The exception, of course, is if the same court later explicitly adopts the newer version in place of the older one. Moreover, if you are using the *Restatement* to fill a gap in the law of the jurisdiction whose law you are researching, it is logical to research the most recent series.

B. Research in *Restatements*

The way legal researchers usually find their way to the *Restatements* is through an initial reference from other sources, not through index searching. Court opinions, law review articles, and treatises are three good sources for providing appropriate and significant *Restatement* sections. Be prudent, however, and consult the index or table of contents for the *Restatement* to which you have a reference to make sure that you are aware of any related sections. To locate a relevant section within a *Restatement*, use the index located in the last topical (non-Appendix) volume of each set. For multi-volume *Restatement* subjects, there may be more than one index to consult involving more than one volume.

To start, pull one of the topical volumes of a *Restatement* (not an Appendix volume) off the shelf and open it to any section. Notice the bold-face font in which the actual *Restatement* provision is printed. Most likely there are also tabulated sections and subsections. You will see a section labeled "Comments." Read this section. The *Restatement* drafters write these comments to explain the provision and identify its limitations. If there is disagreement among the jurisdictions concerning an area of law, the comment will explain why the *Restatement* adopts one position over another. The "Illustrations" sections provide examples of how a particular *Restatement* provision will apply in specific factual situations.

One last tip for the beginning legal researcher: After you have found a *Restatement* section that meets your research needs, study the

"Commentary" in the "Comments" section. Here you can find a wealth of information that can help you construct your legal argument.

To find cases that have cited a particular *Restatement* rule, comment, or illustration, consult the Appendix volumes, which are generally shelved at the end of the topical volumes of the *Restatement*. See Figure 3-3 for *Restatement* treatment of particular cases. The Appendix volumes occupy a lot of shelf space. For example, there are 26 Appendix volumes for the First and Second *Restatement of Torts* alone.[6] The Appendix volumes each cover a specific span of *Restatement* sections (e.g., Sections 403 to 503 of *Torts 2d*). In some newly revised *Restatements*, such as those for *Trusts*, the case citations appear at the end of each section or in pocket parts. Check for both possibilities, in addition to checking the Appendix volumes' span of time (e.g., July 1984 through June 1994 for Sections 403 to 503 of *Torts 2d*). Look up the section in an Appendix volume that lists cases citing the *Restatement* section. See that the "Reporter's Notes" refer you to any changes in the substance of the section. The notes also identify the cases on which the illustrations are based. Case summaries citing the *Restatement* section follow the notes. Following the case summaries are cross-references to West key numbers, *ALR* annotations, and other secondary sources.

Consult the pocket part of every Appendix volume you looked at and any paperbound supplement to determine whether you have found the most up-to-date version of the comments. This will also allow you to find the most recent citations to cases that have cited your *Restatement* section. Multiple volumes of the Appendix may need to be consulted in order to cover the time period from the date of the *Restatement* to the present. Note that some *Restatement* Appendices provide a pocket part at the back of each volume of the Appendix, while others provide a stand-alone pocket part to the last vol-

---

6. Legal researchers beware; the Appendix volumes to the *Second Restatement of Torts* pose special problems. They contain an inaccurate table of contents, inaccurate headers, and organization inconsistencies. In one volume, there is no logical explanation for the section arrangement.

Figure 3-3. *Restatement* Excerpt

§ 341A RESTATEMENT CASE CITATIONS

§ 341A. **Activities Dangerous to Invitees**

C.A.6, 2006. Cit. in disc. Business invitee to corporation's plant who was injured when he was struck by a forklift driven by a plant employee brought negligence action against corporation. The district court granted summary judgment for defendant. This court reversed and remanded upon its reasoning that the district court combined and dismissed two distinct allegations of unreasonable risk of harm, made under the respective theories of ordinary negligence and premises liability, when it dismissed the danger as open and obvious. The court held that defendant, through its employee, owed plaintiff a duty of care to operate its machinery in a reasonably safe manner, and that plaintiff raised an issue of fact as to whether the operation of the forklift in proximity to pedestrians on the loading dock on the day of injury was an open and obvious activity that presented special aspects of danger under Michigan law. Kessler v. Visteon Corp., 448 F.3d 326, 337.

Kan.2005. Cit. and quot. in disc. Parents of minor who was beaten and had his jaw broken in altercation in mobile-home park with fellow park resident and visitor to park sued park owner, among others, for negligence. The trial court granted owner summary judgment. Upon transfer from the court of appeals, this court affirmed, holding, inter alia, that the trial court did not err in finding that owner did not owe a duty to plaintiffs under a premises-liability theory because the harm to minor was unforeseeable. The court concluded that, although owner's attorney had sent a letter to visitor warning him to stay away from the park as a result of an unrelated incident two years earlier, owner had no knowledge that any current problems existed between visitor and minor or that a fight might be taking place. South ex rel. South v. McCarter, 280 Kan. 85, 119 P.3d 1, 8, 11.

plaintiff's claim involving "failure to warn" as a medical-malpractice claim requiring expert testimony. Noting that this claim was akin to a premises-liability claim, the court concluded that technician created a danger to plaintiff by raising the table, and plaintiff's testimony that she could not hear the table being raised and heard no warning to stay on the table created a fact dispute as to whether she should have been aware of the danger. Perkins v. Susan B. Allen Memorial Hosp., 36 Kan.App.2d 885, 146 P.3d 1102, 1108.

Neb.1999. Cit. in headnotes (cit. as § 341), quot. in sup., com. (a) quot. in sup. Attendee at antique vehicles estate sale was severely injured when a hitch ball used in towing vehicles detached, became airborne, and struck him in the head; he brought strict products liability action against manufacturer of hitch ball, and asserted claims of negligence against estate and auctioneers. The trial court entered judgment on a jury verdict for plaintiff. Affirming, this court held that whether the lack of adequate warnings regarding the risks of misusing the hitch ball rendered it unreasonably dangerous was a question of fact properly submitted to the jury; that estate was liable to plaintiff, a business invitee, under a theory of premises liability; and that, even though auctioneers were independent contractors, their liability could be imputed to estate, which retained significant control over their conduct and the auction itself. Haag v. Bongers, 256 Neb. 170, 589 N.W.2d 318, 333-334.

Okl.2004. Cit. in disc. After slipping on waxed floor of walkway between hospital and parking garage, hospital employee sued company that maintained the floor for inadequately warning her of the potentially dangerous condition. Trial court granted company's motion for summary judgment, and ume of the Appendix. Some *Restatements* have softbound supplements. In short, be very careful to consult every book necessary to update your research.

IV. Legal Periodicals

Legal periodicals are an important secondary source in legal research. Some educators suggest starting a legal research query by searching for a legal periodical. There are several reasons for this approach. One is that the foremost legal scholars have written for law school reviews; their articles have been instrumental in shaping the course of many legal doctrines. Another reason is that law review articles usually require the author to bring a particular area of law up to date. Therefore, if the article is recent, a good deal of the research is already done. The last reason for starting with law review articles early in the research process is that they tend to be a motherlode for research footnotes. Even if the law review article is poorly written or was authored by a student, it can still be used as a very valuable research tool for finding citations to cases, statutes, regulations, or other secondary law sources.

A. Types of Legal Periodicals

There are three general types of law journals. The first is the traditional law school, student-edited law review with general coverage of topics. For the last 25 years, there has been a trend in law schools of adding additional scholarly, student-edited journals to their lists of publications. Many times these journals have a subject emphasis such as public policy, international law, urban law, etc. Table 3-4 lists law reviews and journals published by Kansas law schools or bar associations.

Another type of law review or journal is that devoted to one area of the law, published by a professional organization, such as the American Bar Association, or a commercial publisher, such as

Table 3-4. Law Reviews and Journals in Kansas

Title	Publisher
Kansas Law Review	University of Kansas School of Law
Kansas Journal of Law and Public Policy	University of Kansas School of Law
Washburn Law Journal	Washburn University School of Law
Journal of the Kansas Association for Justice	The Legacy of Justice Foundation
Journal of the Kansas Bar Association	Kansas Bar Association

Wolters Kluwer. They are often termed "subject journals" and can vary from the practical to the scholarly. *Trusts and Estates* and the *Insurance Law Journal* are two examples aimed at practicing attorneys in particular fields of law. Many of the articles are written by well known practitioners interpreting recent legislation or court decisions.

The third main type of law journal is that published by bar associations. Each state and the District of Columbia have bar associations. Many larger cities also have bar associations. All of the state and many of the larger city bar associations publish periodicals. The Kansas Bar Association publishes the *Journal of the Kasnsas Bar Association*. The primary purpose is to inform membership of current events, comment on pending and recent legislation, and review local court decisions. The articles tend to be practical, focusing on problem solving. For the researcher, bar association journals tend to be more valuable when researching subjects of current practitioner interest.

B. Indexes for Legal Periodicals

Periodical indexes are available in both print and electronic formats. Two well known, hard copy legal indexes are staples in most law library collections. They are the *Index to Legal Periodicals and Books (ILPB)* and the *Current Law Index (CLI)*. *CLI* is electronically available through Legal Trac (CD-ROM), the *Legal Resources Index* on LexisNexis, or *LRI* on Westlaw. *ILPB* is available from the HW Wilson Company at www.hwwilson.com.

HeinOnline offers free text searching of a growing number of legal journals. A number of law schools subscribe to the service, making it free for their students; the website is www.heinonline.org.

When using *ILPB* or *CLI* in print, go to the latest annual edition to find potential "subject matter headings." After finding the relevant headings, scan over the alphabetical list of titles of articles to find on-point articles. After that, check the latest monthly editions to find more recent on-point articles. Monthly editions 2, 5, 8, and 11 cumulate, so you do not have to check all the monthly editions prior. If you are still looking for on-point articles, check the annual editions going back to 1980. If necessary, check triennial editions before 1980 in *ILPB*. Make certain to update all relevant articles through *Shepard's Citators* or Shepard's online on LexisNexis, or use KeyCite on Westlaw.[7]

V. Treatises

Treatises are simply books with written commentary based on case law and legislation regarding a particular subject. They can be very useful sources of information, depending upon the reliability of the authors, purposes for which the books are intended, and dates of publication. They are recognized with various degrees of authority. Definitive treatises written by persons held in high repute in their particular field are taken very seriously. Some gain a lasting reputation and may be cited as legal authority.

---

7. Updating is covered in Chapter 6.

A. Types of Treatises

Hornbooks are a form of treatise containing "black letter" law. A statement of the law is followed by legal commentary with citation support, commonly of the case law variety. *Newark and Rotunda on Federal Constitutional Law* and *Calamari and Perillo on Contracts* are two examples.

Treatises for the general legal community may be single volumes or multi-volume series. The single-volume variety, if scholarly, may cover the law area in depth. Many continuing legal education (CLE) publications are single-volume books that can be termed treatises, though their treatment of the law is more cursory. These manuals and practice books are usually written to accompany speakers' presentations at certain bar or professional association continuing legal education functions. They may be general sources assisting new attorneys with the basics of particular areas of the law, or they may offer new insights on cutting-edge issues. Some CLE publications of more importance may be indexed and may have a table of cases, a table of statutes, or other finding aids intended for a longer shelf life.

The Kansas Bar Association has published a set of publications called the *Handbooks*. These are practice-oriented treatises covering one legal topic, written by one or more than one author. There is wide coverage of Kansas law in this popular series. The *Handbook* titles are listed below in Table 3-5. Arguably, the highest quality Kansas treatises are those in the seven-volume set called the *Kansas Law and Practice* series published by Thomson/West. Volumes one through six were written by law professors or law emeriti from the University of Kansas School of Law or Washburn University School of Law. Volumes one and two are on Kansas family law, volume three is on Kansas evidence, volumes four through six examine Kansas civil procedure, and the seventh volume is a basic reference authority for Kansas trial practice. The titles of this set are listed below in Table 3-6.

Multi-volume treatises, cyclopedic in nature, may provide exhaustive treatment on a legal topic, documented with statutory and case law with extensive editorial comment. Normally, they are kept

Table 3-5. Kansas Bar Association *Handbooks*

1. Harold H. Houck, *Kansas Construction Law Handbook* (2d ed. 2006). Topeka, Kan.: Kansas Bar Association (KBA Practice Handbook). Available on LexisNexis.
2. Michael A. Barbara, *Kansas Criminal Law Handbook* (4th ed. 2006). Topeka, Kan.: Kansas Bar Association. (KBA Practice Handbook). Available on LexisNexis.
3. Molly M. Wood, *Kansas Long-Term Care Handbook* (1st ed. 1999 with 2001 Supp.). Topeka, Kan.: Kansas Bar Association. (KBA Practice Handbook). Available on LexisNexis.
4. Elinor P. Schroeder, *Kansas Employment Law* (2d ed. 2001). Topeka, Kan.: Kansas Bar Association. (KBA Practice Handbook). Available on LexisNexis.
5. *Kansas Estate Administration Handbook* (6th ed. 1993 with 1997 and 1999 Supps.). Topeka, Kan.: Kansas Bar Association. (KBA Practice Handbook). Available on LexisNexis.
6. Mark F. Anderson et al., *Kansas Ethics Handbook* (1st ed. 1996 with 2001 Supp.). Topeka, Kan.: Kansas Bar Association (KBA Practice Handbook). Available on LexisNexis.
7. Steve Leben et al., *Practitioners Guide to Kansas Family Law* (1st ed. 1997 with 2004 Supp.). Topeka, Kan.: Kansas Bar Association (KBA Practice Handbook). Available on LexisNexis.
8. Joseph A. Custer, *Kansas Legal Research and Reference Guide* (3d ed. 2003). Topeka, Kan.: Kansas Bar Association (KBA Practice Handbook).
9. *Kansas Real Estate Practice and Procedure Handbook* (4th ed. 1999). 2 vols. Topeka, Kan.: Kansas Bar Association (Kansas Practice Handbook). Available on LexisNexis.
10. *Kansas Appellate Practice Handbook* (4th ed. 2007). Topeka, Kan.: Kansas Bar Association (KBA Practice Handbook). Available online at www.kscourts.org/kansas_courts/judicial_council/appellate_practice_handbook/default.asp.
11. Tom Hammond et al., *Kansas Workers' Compensation Practice Manual* (4th ed. 1998 with 2000 Supp.). Topeka, Kan.: Kansas Bar Association. (KBA Practice Handbook). Available on LexisNexis.

Table 3-6. Thomson/West Kansas Practice Series

1. Spencer A. Gard and Robert C. Casad, *Kansas Code of Civil Procedure Annotated* (4th ed., Thomson/West 2003 with 2007 Supp.). Available on Westlaw.
2. Michael A. Barbara, *Lawyers Guide to Kansas Evidence* (5th ed., Thomson/West 2007). Available on Westlaw.
3. James Buchele, *Kansas Family Law* (1st ed., Thomson/West 1999 with 2007 Supp.). 2 vols. Available on Westlaw.
4. Michael A. Barbara, *Lawyer's Guide to Kansas Evidence* (5th ed., Thomson/West 2007). Available on Westlaw.
5. William Sampson et al., *Kansas Trial Handbook* (2d ed., Thomson/West 2006). Available on Westlaw.

up to date by pocket parts, supplements, or superseding volumes. Examples include *McQuillan on Municipal Corporations* and *Collier's Bankruptcy Manual*.

B. Researching in Treatises

There are several ways to find a treatise. One way is to use an online catalog. If you do not know the author of a treatise in a particular law field, you can use the subject field. If a subject search results in too many "hits," you can limit the search by date.

Another good option is a law library's "reserve list" for related law school courses. Some law schools even have this list automated on the online card catalog. Locate the course concerning your subject matter and many times you will get a list of treatises the professor believes are important.

The last good method is to consult the law librarian. Many law librarians are lawyers themselves or have been working as a law librarian so long that they have four-fifths of the library's collection hardwired to their gray matter.

How do you use a treatise after you find one? If using a single-volume treatise, use the index, analysis, or any available tables to find on-point commentary. Make certain you update the treatise with any available supplement or pocket part.

If you have a multi-volume treatise, use the General Index to find the appropriate volume. After finding the appropriate volume, use the volume index or analysis, table of cases, or table of statutes to find on-point sections and pages. Make certain you update the commentary by consulting any supplementation, superseding volumes, or pocket parts.

VI. Uniform Laws

Uniform laws are laws in various subject areas, approved by the National Conference Commissioners on Uniform State Laws, that are often adopted, in whole or nearly whole, by individual states. The best guide to the uniform laws Kansas has adopted is found in *Uniform Laws Annotated* (published by Thomson/West).[8] You can also search a list of those entries having "Uniform" as their first word in the *Kansas Statutes Annotated* (KSA) general index under the heading POPULAR NAME LAWS.

As shown in Table 3-7, Kansas has adopted a number of uniform laws (listed by KSA reference).

---

8. *Uniform Laws Annotated, Master Edition* (Thomson/West 1989) with annual pocket part supplementation. It has annotations to court decisions of every state that referred to the uniform laws. These annotations, reflecting as they do the interpretations of the uniform laws in states that have adopted them, are particularly important for research in states that are considering them or have just recently enacted them. References to secondary sources, including periodical articles, are also provided.

Table 3-7. Uniform Laws Adopted in Kansas

Uniform Law	KSA
Alcoholism and Intoxication Treatment Act	65-4001, et seq.
Anatomical Gift Act (1968 Act)	65-3209, et seq.
Arbitration Act (1955 Act)	5-401, et seq.
Attendance of Witness From Without a State in Criminal Proceedings, Act to Secure	22-4201, et seq.
Certification of Questions of Law (1967)	60-3201, et seq.
Child Custody Jurisdiction Act	38-1301, et seq.
Commercial Code	84-1-101, et seq.
Common Trust Fund Act	9-1069, et seq.
Conservation Easement Act	58-3810, et seq.
Consumer Credit Code (1974)	16a-1-101, et seq.
Consumer Sales Practice Act	50-623, et seq.
Controlled Substances Act (1990)	65-4101, et seq.
Crime Victims Reparations Act	74-7301, et seq.
Criminal Extradition Act	22-2701, et seq.
Declaratory Judgments Act	60-1701, et seq.
Determination of Death Act	77-204, et seq.
Disclaimer of Transfers by Will, Intestacy or Appointment Act	59-2291, et seq.
Disclaimer of Transfers Under Nontestamentary Instruments Act	59-2291, et seq.
Division of Income for Tax Purposes Act	79-3271, et seq.
Durable Power of Attorney Act	58-610, et seq.
Electronic Transactions Act	16-1601, et seq.
Enforcement of Foreign Judgments Act (1964 Act)	60-3001, et seq.
Facsimile Signatures of Public Officials Act	75-4001, et seq.
Federal Lien Registration Act	79-2608, et seq.
Fraudulent Transfer Act	33-201, et seq.
Interstate Family Support Act (1996)	23-9, 101, et seq.
Land Sales Practices Act (Model)	58-3301, et seq.
Limited Partnership Act (1976 Act)	56-122, et seq.
Management of Institutional Funds Act	58-3601, et seq.
Mandatory Disposition of Detainers Act	22-4301, et seq.
Military Justice, Code of	48-2101, et seq.
Nonprobate Transfers on Death Act	59-6a201, et seq.
Notarial Acts, Uniform Law on	53-501, et seq.
Parentage Act (1973 Act)	38-1101, et seq.
Partnership Act (1997 Act)	56-301, et seq.

Table 3-7. Uniform Laws Adopted in Kansas, *continued*

Photographic Copies of Business and Public	
Records as Evidence Act	60-469, et seq.
Premarital Agreement Act	23-801, et seq.
Principal and Income Act (1997 Act)	58-901, et seq.
Rendition of Prisoners as Witnesses in	
Criminal Proceedings Act	22-4207, et seq.
Residential Landlord and Tenant Act	58-2540, et seq.
Securities Act (1956 Act)	17-1252, et seq.
Simplifications of Fiduciary Security	
Transfers Act	17-4903, et seq.
Simultaneous Death Act (1993 Act)	58-708, et seq.
Statutory Rule Against Perpetuities	59-3401, et seq.
Testamentary Additions to Trusts Act (1960)	59-3101, et seq.
TOD Security Registration Act	17-49a01, et seq.
Trade Secrets Act	60-3320, et seq.
Transfers to Minors Act	38-1701, et seq.
Trustees' Power Act	58-1201, et seq.
Unclaimed Property Act (1995 Act)	58-3934, et seq.
Voting by New Residents in Presidential	
Elections Act	25-1801, et seq.

VII. Forms

A lawyer can avoid reinventing the wheel by using a form to write a legal document. There are various form sources available for the Kansas lawyer on both the Internet and in print format. It is very dangerous to merely copy a form verbatim. You will rarely, if ever, find a form that exactly fits the requirements of a legal document that you are drafting. The forms do, however, create a nice starting point, especially if the legal territory being explored is unfamiliar.

When using formbooks, you must thoroughly understand the legal issues that need to be covered in the form. The practice of comparing legal forms and modifying the best forms to meet your specific legal situation is a prudent way to proceed. Hopefully, you will have access to more than one legal form so you can compare and tailor the form to meet the exact parameters of the case in hand. If you have a form and the accompanying state statute to study, the chance of you leaving out an additional cause of action is greatly diminished.

Make certain when using a form that you understand every word of the form. Never assume that the language of a form is appropriate and accurate. Forms do not constitute legal authority and if the terminology is incorrect the meaning of the whole document can be changed. Remember to use the forms as a guide and not as a final draft. Forms tend to be very general and written for a wide audience. If you rely too heavily on a generally worded form, it is all too possible that you will not state enough specific facts in the draft. Thus a motion to dismiss, due to the failure to adequately state a cause of action, could be granted.

Many larger Kansas law libraries contain a variety of formbooks. Even smaller law libraries in Kansas will usually have a recognized formbook or two to use. There are several formbooks available in print for attorneys to use covering Kansas and other states or the federal jurisdictions. There are also a growing number of forms available electronically. Several Kansas district courts, for example, have forms available on their websites. A caveat for those using online forms: make sure that they are legitimate and do not use them exclusively when drafting.

A "formbook" may provide actual forms or suggested language that can be crafted into a form. Examples of Kansas formbooks include *Kansas Judicial Council Probate Forms* and *Vernon's Kansas Forms with Practice Commentaries: Legal Business and Procedural Forms Keyed to the General Statutes*. Federal forms are available in numerous titles, including *Federal Procedural Forms, Lawyers Edition* and *West's Federal Forms*. Search the online library catalog for topical formbooks.

You can gain access to business forms online at the secretary of state website (www.kssos.org/forms/forms.html). Online Kansas court forms are available at the Kansas Judicial Council website (www.kscourts.org/council).

VIII. Secondary Source Final Tips

- Never cite to legal encyclopedias as primary authority. They consist of very general introductory narrative. There is no in-depth analysis of a legal issue. The researcher can find *Am Jur 2d* online in LexisNexis and Westlaw.
- *ALRs* are truly hit or miss legal research propositions. Unlike legal encyclopedias, they do not cover all or close to all legal issues. They tend to cover the novel, curious, and newly breaking legal topics. If your research issue is covered by *ALR*, you will be aided in finding Kansas law through the *Table of Jurisdictions*. Like legal encyclopedias, they do not contain in-depth analysis.
- *Restatements* can be very helpful for researching common law topics. They can help you find mandatory and persuasive authority for adopted *Restatement* sections in Kansas. Selected *Restatements* are available through LexisNexis and Westlaw.
- Legal periodicals can be very useful in gaining background information, some very analytical. They can be an abundance for citations to authority. They can take the form of providing in-depth analysis of a narrow topic, newly breaking topic or an undeveloped area of the law. The finding aid print indexes, *ILPB* and *CLI,* are both available online. Both LexisNexis and Westlaw have databases of legal periodicals that can also be searched in full-text format, either in individual publication databases or in combined secondary source databases.
- Treatises are best used as an in-depth discussion and analysis of one particular area of the law. They can also be very helpful in finding primary authority citations. LexisNexis and Westlaw have added several treatises over the past several years.
- The commentary accompanying uniform laws can be very helpful in interpreting law adopted by the Kansas legislature. They can also be very helpful in finding persuasive authority from other jurisdictions adopting a particular restate-

ment. The print source, *Uniform Laws Annotated, Master Index*, is a great source for locating uniform laws. A Kansas researcher can also search a list of those entries having "Uniform" as their first word in the KSA general index under POPULAR NAME LAWS. Uniform laws are also searchable on LexisNexis and Westlaw.

Chapter 4

Judicial Opinions and Reporters

A judicial opinion, also called a case, is written by a court to explain its decision in a particular dispute. Not all litigation produces a written judicial opinion. Jury trials, for example, do not typically result in a written judicial opinion. Furthermore, not all written judicial opinions become precedent. Only cases that the court designates for publication become binding, mandatory authority.[1] Cases designated for publication are printed in rough chronological order in books called *reporters*.[2] These print case reporters therefore function as gatekeepers in the common law system; only cases found on their pages are "the law." Although online resources are gradually eroding this paradigm,[3] even researchers working primarily with online resources must be familiar with reporters because they often dictate case citation formats and pagination. Also, in the event of conflicting texts, the print version will likely trump the electronic version.

Reliable and timely case reporting has played an important role in the American legal system. Early in the nation's history, lawyers and judges borrowed heavily from the English common law to argue and decide cases. The use of English precedent gradually faded as the

---

1. Individual courts often have rules regarding the publication of cases. For example, the publication of Kansas appellate cases is governed by Kansas Supreme Court Rule 7.04.

2. Chapter 5 explains how to use *digests* that index cases by topic.

3. Online publication of "unpublished" decisions is beginning to undermine the historical importance of publication in print reporters. *See e.g.* Fed. R. App. P. 32.1 (authorizing litigants in the federal Courts of Appeals to cite unpublished opinions of those courts beginning in 2007, but allowing courts to determine the weight of unpublished opinions).

United States began to develop its own body of case law. Attorneys needed reliable access to these cases and pioneering legal publishers began to compete for their dollar. Eventually, relatively standardized formatting and publication patterns emerged and the print case reporter became ingrained in the American common law system. The West Publishing Company played an important role in this evolution, with its comprehensive *National Reporter System* largely setting the template for modern court decisions.

Reporters in West's *National Reporter System* are examples of *commercial reporters*. Commercial reporters are printed by private legal publishers with market incentives for timeliness and editorial enhancements. In contrast, *official reporters* are published by the government, typically do not offer many editorial enhancements, and often lag several years behind their commercial counterparts. This distinction has blurred in recent decades as many states have adopted commercial reporters as official reporters.[4] Kansas state cases, however, continue to be published in both official reporters and commercial reporters.

The coverage of a reporter may be based on court, region, or topic. Some reporters include only cases decided by a certain court, for example, the Kansas Supreme Court. Other reporters include cases from courts within a specific geographic region, for example, the western United States. Still other reporters publish only those cases that deal with a certain topic, such as bankruptcy, media law, or rules of civil and criminal procedure. Reporters that publish cases from a particular court or geographic area are the most commonly used by general practitioners and are the focus of this chapter.

This chapter begins with an overview of the Kansas and federal court systems. Then it explains reporters and online sources that provide the text of Kansas and federal cases.

---

4. In addition, West's *Federal Reporter* and *Federal Supplement* have long served as de facto official reporters for the United States Courts of Appeals and the United States District Courts, respectively.

I. Court Systems

The basic American court structure includes a trial court, an intermediate court of appeals, and an ultimate appellate court, often called the "supreme" court.[5] These courts exist at both the state and federal levels.

A. Kansas Courts

The trial courts of Kansas are called district courts, and they have general, original jurisdiction over all civil and criminal cases.[6] The state's 105 counties are divided into 31 judicial districts, with a district court in each county. Both jury trials and bench trials take place in the district courts. Litigants may appeal adverse decisions to the Kansas Court of Appeals and, in some circumstances, to the Kansas Supreme Court.

Kansas's intermediate appellate court, the Kansas Court of Appeals, has a bifurcated history. In 1895 the first Court of Appeals of Kansas was created, but it was abolished in 1901. The current Kansas Court of Appeals came into being in 1977. It is located in Topeka in the Kansas Judicial Center, although hearings are often held throughout the state. The Court of Appeals hears all appeals from the district courts in both civil and criminal cases, except those that may be appealed directly to the Supreme Court. The Court may hear appeals *en banc* but usually sits in panels of three judges.

---

5. The following description omits for brevity municipal courts and tribal courts. Information about Kansas municipal courts, including links to those courts that maintain websites, can be found at www.kscourts.org/kansas-courts/municipal-courts/default.asp. Information on tribal courts is available at the Tribal Court Clearinghouse website: www.tribal-institute.org/index.htm. In addition, VersusLaw (www.versuslaw.com) offers tribal law resources and is working toward the creation of a comprehensive online tribal court database.

6. This is true except in instances where original jurisdiction lies with an appellate court.

The state court of last resort, the Kansas Supreme Court, sits in Topeka in the Kansas Judicial Center. It hears appeals in any case in which a statute has been held unconstitutional as well as direct appeals from the district courts in the most serious criminal cases. It may review cases decided by the Court of Appeals and also has original jurisdiction in several types of cases. The Kansas Supreme Court also possesses general administrative authority over the practicing bench and bar in Kansas. The Kansas Judicial Branch website (www.kscourts.org) is an invaluable resource for more detailed information about Kansas courts and also provides links to individual court websites.

B. Federal Courts

In the federal judicial system, the trial courts are called United States District Courts. There are ninety-four district courts in the federal system, with each district drawn from a particular state. A state with a relatively small population might not be subdivided into smaller geographic regions. The entire state of Kansas, for example, makes up the federal District of Kansas. Even so, district courts are located in three cities: Kansas City, Topeka, and Wichita. States with larger populations and higher caseloads are subdivided into more districts. For example, Oklahoma has three federal districts: eastern, northern, and western.

Intermediate appellate courts in the federal system are called United States Courts of Appeals. There are courts of appeals for each of the thirteen federal circuits. Twelve of these circuits are based on geographic jurisdiction. Eleven numbered circuits cover all the states; the twelfth is the District of Columbia Circuit. The thirteenth federal circuit, called the Federal Circuit, hears appeals from district courts in all other circuits on issues related to patent law and from certain specialized courts and agencies. A map showing the federal circuits is available at www.uscourts.gov/courtlinks. Circuit maps may also be found in the front of the *Federal Reporter* and the *Federal Supplement*, reporters that publish the cases decided by federal courts.

Kansas is in the Tenth Circuit. This means that cases from the United States District Court for the District of Kansas are appealed to the United States Court of Appeals for the Tenth Circuit. This circuit encompasses Colorado, Kansas, New Mexico, Oklahoma, Utah, and Wyoming.

The highest court in the federal system is the United States Supreme Court. It often decides cases concerning the United States Constitution and federal statutes, although U.S. Const. Art. III, § 2 and 28 U.S.C. § 1251 et seq. extend its jurisdiction to a wide variety of cases and controversies. Parties who wish to have the U.S. Supreme Court hear their case must file a petition for *certiorari,* as the court has discretion over which cases it hears and typically "grants cert." to only a small fraction of these petitions.

The website for the federal judiciary contains maps, court addresses, explanations of jurisdiction, and other helpful information. The address is www.uscourts.gov.

C. Courts of Other States

Most states have the three-tier court system of Kansas and the federal judiciary. A few do not have an intermediate appellate court, just as Kansas did not during much of the twentieth century. Another difference in some court systems is that the "supreme" court is not the highest court. In New York, for example, the trial courts are called supreme courts and the highest court is the Court of Appeals.

Citation manuals are good references for learning the names and hierarchy of the courts, as well as for learning proper citation to legal authorities. The two most popular are the *ALWD Citation Manual: A Professional System of Citation,* written by Dean Darby Dickerson and the Association of Legal Writing Directors,[7] and *The Bluebook: A Uniform System of Citation,* written by students from several law schools.[8] Both manuals provide tables with information on federal and state courts.[9]

---

7. ALWD & Darby Dickerson, *ALWD Citation Manual* (3d ed., Aspen Publishers 2006) ("*ALWD Manual*").

8. *The Bluebook: A Uniform System of Citation* (The Columbia Law Review et al. eds., 18th ed., The Harvard Law Review Assn. 2005) ("*Bluebook*").

9. See Appendix A for more information regarding citation.

Table 4-1. Print Reporters for Kansas Cases

Reporter	Citation Abbreviation	Coverage
Kansas Reports	Kan.	Kansas Supreme Court, 1862-date
Kansas Court of Appeals Reports (First & Second Series)	Kan. App. Kan. App. 2d	Kansas Court of Appeals, 1895-1901 1977-date
Pacific Reporter (First, Second, & Third Series)	P., P.2d, P.3d	Kansas Supreme Court, 1883-date Kansas Court of Appeals, 1895-1901 1977-date

II. Reporters for Kansas Cases

Cases from state trial courts in Kansas are not published; in fact, few states publish opinions at the trial court level. The courthouse and the Internet are typically the two best options for obtaining any decisions issued by Kansas district courts. Legal researchers in Kansas are typically interested in cases decided by the Kansas Supreme Court or the Kansas Court of Appeals. Table 4-1 summarizes the major reporters in which these cases are published. This table will also be a useful reference for the following discussion, which traces such a case chronologically through the publication process.

A. Slip Opinions

Before a case is printed in a reporter, it is a *slip opinion*. A slip opinion is the actual document produced by the court, without the editorial enhancements normally added by legal publishers. Slip opinions are traditionally obtained in print from the courthouse, although they now promptly appear online at both official and commercial websites. Additionally, some law libraries in Kansas continue to receive hard copies of slip opinions from the Kansas appellate courts.

The "Recent and Published Opinions" link at the Kansas Judicial Branch website (www.kscourts.org) offers access to recent slip opinions issued by the Kansas Supreme Court and Kansas Court of Appeals. A more comprehensive collection of Kansas state and federal law is available for members of the Kansas Bar Association via Casemaker (www.ksbar.org/casemaker). The full text of Kansas cases is also available from online services like FindLaw (www.findlaw.com), LexisOne (www.lexisone.com), Loislaw (www.loislaw.com), and VersusLaw (www.versuslaw.com). FindLaw and LexisOne are currently free.[10] Loislaw and VersusLaw require paid subscriptions, but they are less expensive than LexisNexis or Westlaw, which also offer up-to-date access to slip opinions. These commercial databases typically provide unique citations to slip opinions that can be used until the print reporter citations become available.

If a Kansas appellate case is not designated for publication, it will be available only as a slip opinion and will not be published in reporters or their advance sheets.[11] Keep in mind that unpublished opinions from the Kansas Supreme Court, Kansas Court of Appeals, and Kansas federal courts can be a rich source of discussion of Kansas legal questions not clearly answered in published cases. In 2007, for example, the Court of Appeals decided 1,343 cases, but 88% of them were unpublished. Even the Kansas Supreme Court issued 126 unpublished opinions in 2007, or 48% of its total opinions. Over a period of years, a great many questions are decided in these unpublished decisions. But even when you find an answer in such a case, your creativity as a lawyer still must be brought to bear on the situation because usually unpublished decisions do not constitute binding precedent on later courts.[12]

B. Advance Sheets

Legal publishers gather slip opinions and compile them chronologically in softbound booklets called *advance sheets*, which can be

---

10. LexisOne requires registration to access free case law.

11. However, both *Pacific Reporter* and the official Kansas reporters provide tables listing unpublished opinions.

12. *See* Kan. S. Ct. R. 7.04(f); D. Kan. R. 7.6(b); and Fed. R. App. P. 32.1.

published much more quickly than hardbound books. The pagination in the advance sheets is identical to the hardbound volumes; thus, a cite to a case in the advance sheets will still be accurate after the case is published in hardbound volumes. West publishes advance sheets for *Pacific Reporter* on a weekly basis. The Kansas government publishes *Advance Sheets of the Kansas Supreme Court and Kansas Court of Appeals* in every month except February, June, August, and October.

In addition to cases, advance sheets also contain helpful tables and indexes. Some of the features found in *Pacific Reporter* advance sheets include lists and summaries of the cases reported in the current issue, summaries of important decisions from around the nation, parallel citation tables, Words and Phrases updating, and a *Key Number Digest* for the current issue.[13] Similarly, *Advance Sheets of the Kansas Supreme Court and Kansas Court of Appeals* include lists of published and unpublished cases, and a subject index. Most of these tables and indexes, along with several other useful features, can also be found in hardbound reporters.

C. Commercial Reporters

Kansas Reports and *Kansas Court of Appeals Reports*, discussed below in Section II.D., are the official reporters for Kansas appellate cases and are published by the state government. However, it often takes years for the final hardbound volumes to arrive on the shelves. To fill in this time-gap, cases from these courts are reported more promptly in a commercially produced *regional reporter* called *Pacific Reporter*. While the text of the court's opinion is the same in the official and regional reporters, the appearance and editorial enhancements are different. Most importantly, *Pacific Reporter* includes headnotes with *topic and key number* information that integrates the cases within the *American Digest System*. These features are discussed at length in Chapter 5. For now, simply note that these features allow researchers to quickly locate similar cases and that these features are not found in the official reporters.

---

13. *See* Chapter 5 for a more detailed explanation of Words and Phrases and the *Key Number Digest*.

To cite a Kansas case in *Pacific Reporter*, include the name of the case, the volume number, the reporter abbreviation, and the page number. Then in a parenthetical, include an abbreviation to show that a Kansas court decided the case and the date the case was decided. For example: *Rose v. Via Christi Health System, Inc.*, 113 P.3d 241 (Kan. 2005). This case is reported in volume 113 of the series *Pacific Reporter, Third Series*, beginning on page 241. The case was decided in 2005 by the Kansas Supreme Court.[14]

Regional reporters publish several courts' opinions under a single title. *Pacific Reporter* publishes cases from the courts of the following fifteen states: Alaska, Arizona, California, Colorado, Hawaii, Idaho, Kansas, Montana, Nevada, New Mexico, Oklahoma, Oregon, Utah, Washington, and Wyoming. *Pacific Reporter* includes cases from the intermediate and highest appellate courts of most of these states.[15]

Pacific Reporter is part of West's *National Reporter System*. Other regional reporters in the *National Reporter System* are *North Eastern Reporter*, *Atlantic Reporter*, *South Eastern Reporter*, *Southern Reporter*, *South Western Reporter*, and *North Western Reporter*. The states whose cases are included in each of these regional reporters are listed in Table 4-2.

Sometimes when a reporter reaches a certain volume number, the publisher begins another series. In 1931, after volume 300 of *Pacific Reporter* was published, the publisher decided to begin again with volume one of *Pacific Reporter, Second Series*. In 2000, following publication of volume 999 in the second series, a third series was started, *Pacific Reporter, Third Series*. When citing the *Rose* case discussed earlier, the abbreviation "P.3d" shows that the case appears in the third series rather than an earlier one.

West also publishes a variation on the theme of *Pacific Reporter* entitled *Kansas Cases*. This series is an "off-print" reporter that strips all

---

14. The formatting for case names will be different for various citation styles (see Appendix A for more information regarding citations).

15. Since 1960, opinions of California's intermediate appellate courts have been published in *California Reporter*, not in *Pacific Reporter*.

Table 4-2. Regional Reporters and States Included

Atlantic Reporter (A., A.2d)	Connecticut, Delaware, the District of Columbia, Maine, Maryland, New Hampshire, New Jersey, Pennsylvania, Rhode Island, and Vermont
North Eastern Reporter (N.E., N.E.2d)	Illinois, Indiana, Massachusetts, New York, and Ohio
North Western Reporter (N.W., N.W.2d)	Iowa, Michigan, Minnesota, Nebraska, North Dakota, South Dakota, and Wisconsin
Pacific Reporter (P., P.2d, P.3d)	Alaska, Arizona, California, Colorado, Hawaii, Idaho, Kansas, Montana, Nevada, New Mexico, Oklahoma, Oregon, Utah, Washington, and Wyoming
South Eastern Reporter (S.E., S.E.2d)	Georgia, North Carolina, South Carolina, Virginia, and West Virginia
South Western Reporter (S.W., S.W.2d, S.W.3d)	Arkansas, Kentucky, Missouri, Tennessee, and Texas
Southern Reporter (So., So. 2d, So. 3d)	Alabama, Florida, Louisiana, and Mississippi

non-Kansas cases out of the *Pacific Reporter*. All formatting, editorial enhancements, pagination, and citation remain identical to *Pacific Reporter*.

D. Official Reporters

After appearing in slip opinions, advance sheets, and regional reporters, published cases decided by the Kansas Supreme Court eventually appear in hardbound *Kansas Reports*. The abbreviation for this reporter is "Kan." To continue the earlier example, the case *Rose v. Via Christi Health System, Inc.*, 279 Kan. 523 (2005), can be found in volume 279 of the series *Kansas Reports*, starting on page 523. The case was decided in 2005.

Modern Kansas intermediate appellate court opinions are published in a separate reporter entitled *Kansas Court of Appeals Reports*,

Second. "Kan. App. 2d" is the abbreviation for this reporter. The case *Alexander v. Everhart,* 27 Kan. App. 2d 897 (2000), was published in volume 27 of the series *Kansas Court of Appeals Reports, Second,* beginning on page 897. It was decided in 2000. Cases decided from 1895–1901 by the first Court of Appeals of Kansas were published in *Kansas Court of Appeals Reports,* volumes 1 through 10.

E. Features of a Reported Case

A case printed in a reporter (or available through an online service) contains the exact language of the court's opinion. Additionally, publishers add editorial enhancements intended to aid researchers in learning about the case. Some of these research aids are gleaned from the court record of the case, while others are written by the publisher's editorial staff. The following discussion explains the information and enhancements included in *Pacific Reporter.*

To best understand the following discussion, select from the library shelves a volume of *Pacific Reporter,* preferably a volume containing a case you are familiar with. Alternatively, refer to the case excerpt in Figure 4-3 for examples of the features found in the print version of *Pacific Reporter.* Figure 4-4 shows the same case as it appears on Westlaw. Note that the editorial enhancements will be different in official Kansas reporters or non-West electronic databases, although the text of the actual opinion will be identical.

Parties and procedural designations. At the beginning of the case, all of the parties are listed with their procedural designations.

Docket numbers. The number assigned to the case by a court is called a docket number. Docket numbers are helpful in locating the parties' briefs, a court's orders, or other documents related to that case. While some of these documents can be found in commercial databases, often they can be obtained only from the court that decided the case.

Court and date information. The name of the court that decided the case, and the date it was decided, can be found directly below the docket number.

Figure 4-3, Part I. Case Excerpt from *Pacific Reporter*

ROSE v. VIA CHRISTI HEALTH SYSTEM   Kan. **241**

Cite as 113 P.3d 241 (Kan. 2005)

1. Appeal and Error ⬖854(1)

Supreme Court could affirm trial court ruling in wrongful death action even though trial court failed to cite to any authority to support its ruling, as result was correct.

2. Appeal and Error ⬖854(2)

If a trial court reaches the right result, its decision will be upheld even though the trial court relied upon the wrong ground or assigned erroneous reasons for its decision; the reason given by the trial court for its ruling is immaterial if the result is correct.

Aldena M. ROSE, Individually and as Surviving Spouse of Lyle Rose, Deceased, and Marilyn A. Corr, as Executor of the Estate of Lyle Rose, Deceased, Appellants/Cross-appellees,

v.

VIA CHRISTI HEALTH SYSTEM, INC./ ST. FRANCIS CAMPUS, Appellee/Cross-appellant.

No. 88,434.

Supreme Court of Kansas.

June 3, 2005.

Background: Executor of estate of deceased patient brought a negligence action against hospital, after patient died as a result of injuries sustained from falling out of hospital bed. After a judgment in executor's favor, hospital moved to offset judgment by the medical expenses it wrote off for patient pursuant to contract with Medicare. The Sedgwick District Court, Warren M. Wilbert, J., granted hospital's motion. On cross-appeals, the Supreme Court affirmed in part and reversed in part, 276 Kan. 539, 78 P.3d 798.

Holdings: On rehearing, the Supreme Court, Luckert, J., modified its prior opinion and held that:

(1) offset did not abrogate Medicare's right to subrogation, and

(2) hospital was entitled post-judgment setoff.

Affirmed.

Allegrucci, J., dissented with opinion in which Davis, J., joined.

3. Death ⬖91

Trial court's decision that health care provider, which was also Medicare provider, was entitled to offset proportionate share of the medical expenses portion of the judgment against it in wrongful death action by the amount that Medicare did not pay did not abrogate Medicare's right to subrogation; provider did not seek to diminish plaintiff's recovery by that portion of the jury verdict representing the amount paid by Medicare, which was the amount subject to Medicare's subrogation claim.

4. States ⬖18.5

If a state trial court's ruling conflicts with federal law, that ruling will be without effect under the Supremacy Clause of the United States Constitution. U.S.C.A. Const. Art. 6, cl. 2.

5. Appeal and Error ⬖842(1)

Statutory interpretation is a question of law, and review is unlimited.

6. Statutes ⬖181(1), 190

The fundamental rule of statutory construction to which all other rules are subordinate is that the intent of the legislature governs if that intent can be ascertained, and when a statute is plain and unambiguous, the court must give effect to the intention of the legislature as expressed rather than determine what the law should or should not be.

Source: *Pacific Reporter, Third Series*. Reprinted with permission of Thomson Reuters/West.

4 · Judicial Opinions and Reporters   71

Figure 4-4. Case Excerpt from Westlaw

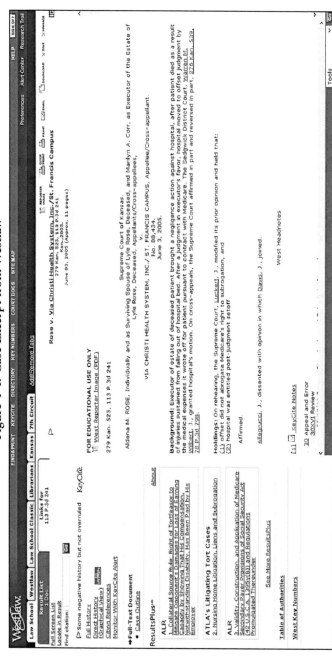

Source: Westlaw. Reprinted with permission of Thomson Reuters/West.

Background information. This information is a brief synopsis of the case prepared by the editors at West. This feature should never be quoted or cited as authority. Beware of the distinction between this synopsis and the official *Syllabus of the Court*, which may be cited.

Holdings. This is another editorial enhancement created by West's editors. The background information caveats apply equally to this feature.

Headnotes. A headnote is a sentence or short paragraph that sets out a single point of law in a case. Most cases will have several headnotes. The text of each headnote often closely tracks the text of the opinion. But because only the opinion itself is authoritative, do not cite headnotes in legal documents. At the beginning of each headnote is a number identifying it in sequence with other headnotes. Within the text of the opinion, the same sequence number will appear in brackets (or sometimes bold print) at the point in the text supporting the headnote. Read and cite that text, not the headnote.

Headnotes are the product of a given publisher's editorial staff. Thus, the number of headnotes—and the text of the headnotes—may differ depending on which publisher's reporter is being used. The headnotes found in *Pacific Reporter* include topic and key number information that allows researchers to quickly locate similar cases.[16] Moreover, the headnotes in *Pacific Reporter* will be the same as those on Westlaw. Headnotes found on LexisNexis, though, are part of an entirely separate system.

Syllabus by the Court. This outline of the decision was prepared by the court, and therefore can be cited and quoted.[17]

Attorney information. The names of the attorneys who argued the case are listed before the official text of the opinion.

---

16. The case-finding function of headnotes is discussed extensively in Chapter 5.

17. *See* K.S.A. 20-111 ("When a case is decided by the supreme court, the judge delivering the opinion shall, at the time the decision is made, file with the clerk a brief statement, in writing, of the points decided in the case, which shall constitute the syllabus in the published reports of the case.")

Opinion. The official text of the opinion of the court follows the attorney information, preceded by the name of the judge who wrote the opinion.

If the judges who heard the case do not agree on the outcome or the reasons for the outcome, there may be several opinions. The opinion supported by a majority of the judges is called the *majority opinion.* An opinion written to agree with the outcome but not the reasoning of the majority is called a *concurring opinion.* Opinions written by judges who disagree with the outcome supported by the majority of judges are called *dissenting opinions.* While only the majority opinion is binding precedent, the other opinions provide valuable insights and may be cited as persuasive authority. If there is no majority on both the outcome and the reasoning, the case will be decided by whichever opinion garners the most support, and is called a *plurality decision.*

F. Kansas Cases on LexisNexis and Westlaw

LexisNexis and Westlaw provide the full text of Kansas cases (including both published and unpublished cases) soon after they are decided, with editorial enhancements appearing soon thereafter. Cases found on Westlaw will have editorial enhancements based upon West's *National Reporter System,* including headnotes with topic-key numbers that are part of the *American Digest System.* Cases found on LexisNexis will have different editorial enhancements, including LexisNexis headnotes. If you have a citation for a Kansas case, you can retrieve the case using "Get a Document" on LexisNexis or "Find by citation" on Westlaw.

When working with cases from any online provider, be aware of pagination markers because information usually must be cited to a specific page in the print reporter. To show where a page change occurs, online providers use *star paging.* Whenever text in the print reporter runs to the next page, that page number will be embedded in the text of the online version and preceded by an asterisk or "star." To give star pagination for multiple reporters, an online provider will assign a different number of stars to each reporter. Whenever a certain reporter changes pages, the new page number will follow the related number of stars. Figure 4-5 shows a LexisNexis case with star paging.

Figure 4-5. Star Paging on LexisNexis

LexisNexis® Total Research System　　　Custom ID ▼ : No Description | Switch Client | Preferences | User Support | Sign Out | Help

Search | Research Tasks | Get a Document | Shepard's® | Alerts | Total Litigator | Transactional Advisor | Counsel Selector

FOCUS™ Terms

View: Case Brief | Full | Custom

Search Within | Original Results (1 - ...) ▼ | Go | Advanced

More Like This | More Like Selected Text | Shepardize® | TOA
◁ 1 of 1 ▷　　　FAST Print | Print | Download | Fax | Email | Text Only
Pages: 15

△ Rose v. Via Christi Health Sys., Inc., 279 Kan. 523 (Copy w/ Cite)

omitted.]" *Sobriett v. The Haskell Co.*, 270 Kan. 95, 100-01, 12 P.3d 411 (2000).

[*527] The legislature is presumed to have expressed its intent through the language of the statutory scheme it enacted. *State ex rel. Stovall v. Meneley*, 271 Kan. 355, 378, 22 P.3d 124 (2001) (citing *In re Marriage of Killman*, 264 Kan. 33, 42-43, 955 P.2d 1228 (1998)). Words and phrases that have acquired a peculiar and appropriate meaning in law are to be construed accordingly. *Galindo v. City of Coffeyville*, 256 Kan. 455, 465, 885 P.2d 1246 (1994).

Applying these rules, we begin the analysis by determining what Congress intended when it stated a provider may not "charge" a beneficiary with [***9] an unreimbursed amount. The word "charge" has a particularized meaning, the effect of which is to constrain a provider's ability to treat the unreimbursed expenses as a debt of the beneficiary. See *Black's Law Dictionary* 227 (7th ed. 1999) ("charge" means "to impose a lien or claim; to encumber; to demand a fee; to bill"). Moreover, as other courts have concluded, HN4 the Medicare statute does not specifically address situations where the tortfeasor is the substance abuser. ... See, e.g., *Joiner v. Medical Center East, Inc.*, 709 So.2d 1209, 1221 (Ala. 1998) (health care provider can assert lien against injured party's reimbursement from primary insurance, including amounts required by Medicare to be "written off").

In this case, the trial court's order adjusted the verdict to reflect the measure [**245] of damages to which Rose was entitled under Kansas law and was not, in a technical sense, a "charge" where the amount was treated as a debt [***10] owed by Rose. HN5 The basic principle of damages is to make a party whole by putting the party back in the same position as if the injury had not occurred, not to grant a windfall. *State ex rel. Stephan v. Wolfenbarger & McCulley, P.A.*, 236 Kan. 183, Syl. P 4, 690 P.2d 380 (1984); see 25 C.J.S. Damages § 3, pp. 627-29 (quoted in *Thurston v. Haward-Needles-Tammen & Bergendoff*, 234 Kan. 289, 301, 672 P.2d 1083 (1983) [Schroeder, C.J., dissenting]). If a defendant has paid the loss in some way, the defendant should not be required to pay again. This principle is adopted in [*528] the *Restatement (Second) of Torts § 920A* (1977), which this court found consistent with Kansas common-law principles. *Harper v. Gerdel*, 242 Kan. 798, 800, 751 P.2d 1038 (1988). The *Restatement (Second) of Torts § 920A* provides:

"(1) A payment made by a tortfeasor or by a person acting for him to a person whom he has injured is credited against his tort liability, as are payments made by another who is, or believes he is, subject to the same tort liability.

"(2) Payment made to or benefits [***11] conferred on the injured party from other sources are not credited against the tortfeasor's liability, although they cover all or a part of the harm for which the tortfeasor is liable."

Consistent with the rule stated in the *Restatement (Second) of Torts § 920A(1)*, in *Hustead v. Bendix Corp.*, 233 Kan. 870, 877-78, 666 P.2d 1175 (1983), this court considered the effect of a partial payment of damages predicated upon possible tort liability. The court held that HN6 the advance or partial payment was not admissible into evidence under K.S.A. 40-275. The court continued, stating: "Such a payment constitutes a credit and may be deducted from any settlement or final judgment rendered." 233 Kan. at 878.

In this regard, it is important to note that the *Restatement (Second) of Torts § 920A(1)* and our statements of the rule speak of the tortfeasor being allowed a "credit" rather than an "offset" for the damages paid. The distinction, though seemingly minor, is technically very important. HN7 The right of setoff (also called "offset") allows entities that owe each other [***12] money to apply their mutual debts against each other, thereby avoiding "the absurdity of making A pay B when B owes A." *Studley v. Boylston Nat. Bank*, 229 U.S. 523, 528, 57 L. Ed. 1313, 33 S. Ct. 806 (1913)." *Citizens Bank of Maryland v. Strumpf*, 516 U.S. 16, 18, 133 L. Ed. 2d 258, 116 S. Ct. 286 (1995). Compare that situation to a circumstance where a tortfeasor gratuitously provides a benefit to the plaintiff; the plaintiff owes no debt. The tortfeasor could not "charge" the victim or seek an offset for the benefits which the tortfeasor conferred upon the plaintiff. See *Restatement (Second) of Torts § 920A*, comments

Table 4-6. Reporters for Federal Court Cases

Court	Reporter Name	Abbreviation
U.S. Supreme Court	*United States Reports* (official)	U.S.
	Supreme Court Reporter	S. Ct.
	United States Supreme Court Reports, Lawyers' Edition	L. Ed. or L. Ed. 2d
U.S. Courts of Appeals	*Federal Reporter*	F. or F.2d or F.3d
	Federal Appendix (unpublished cases)	Fed. Appx.
U.S. District Courts	*Federal Supplement*	F. Supp. or F. Supp. 2d
	Federal Rules Decisions	F.R.D.

III. Reporters for Federal Cases

So far this chapter has dealt with reporters for Kansas and other states courts. This part explains the reporters for cases decided by federal courts. Table 4-6 lists the federal court reporters, along with their citation abbreviations.

A. United States Supreme Court Cases

Decisions of the United States Supreme Court are reported in *United States Reports*, which is the official reporter; *Supreme Court Reporter*, published by West; and *United States Supreme Court Reports, Lawyers' Edition*, now part of the LexisNexis family. Citation to the official *United States Reports* is preferred but that series typically publishes bound volumes several years after the cases were decided. Thus, for recent cases, researchers often use the more timely commercial reporters. Another source for finding recent cases from the Supreme Court is *United States Law Week*. This service publishes the full text of cases from the Supreme Court and provides summaries of important decisions of state and federal courts.

The importance of Supreme Court opinions means they can be found in numerous places online. The Court's website at www.supremecourtus.gov offers slip opinions soon after the decisions are rendered, and often provides supplementary material such as briefs and oral argument transcripts. An educational site supported by Cornell University also provides decisions quickly. The address is http://supct.law.cornell.edu/supct. Both LexisNexis and Westlaw provide quick access to Supreme Court opinions, as well as to briefs filed by the parties.

B. United States Courts of Appeals Cases

Cases decided by the federal intermediate appellate courts are published in *Federal Reporter*, now in its third series. The abbreviations for these reporters are F., F.2d, and F.3d, depending on the series. Federal appeals courts maintain their own websites that provide access to recent cases for free. A gateway to each court is available at www.uscourts.gov. A great deal of variation exists between court websites, but all are invaluable sources of information.

Both LexisNexis and Westlaw include cases for federal courts of appeals in several databases. Be careful, however: both of these services provide access to cases that are "unpublished." If a case does not have a citation to *Federal Reporter*, the case may be of limited authority in some jurisdictions. Some Court of Appeals cases that were not selected for publication in *Federal Reporter* can be found in a relatively new reporter series, *Federal Appendix*. While it is somewhat paradoxical that the *Federal Appendix* is a reporter dedicated to printing unpublished decisions, it is indicative of the growing importance of unpublished decisions (discussed above in Section II.A.). With a proper understanding of their limitations, unpublished decisions can be valuable persuasive authority in certain situations.

C. United States District Courts Cases

Unlike most state trial courts, selected cases from the United States District Courts are published. Those cases selected for publication are reported in *Federal Supplement* and *Federal Supplement, Second Series*. The citation abbreviations for these reporters are F. Supp. and F. Supp. 2d. Some cases decided by U.S. District Courts addressing the Federal Rules of Civil Procedure and Federal Rules of Criminal Procedure can be found in *Federal Rules Decisions*. The citation abbreviation for this reporter is F.R.D. Some opinions are available on the U.S. Courts and Cornell websites as well. LexisNexis and Westlaw tend to make available more U.S. District Court cases, so remember the caveat about the authoritative value of "unpublished" decisions.

IV. Reading and Analyzing Cases

This chapter has explained how cases are systematically printed and published in rough chronological order. Finding a relevant case among the thousands published every year is often akin to finding a needle in a haystack, and that difficult task is discussed in the following chapter. However, after locating a relevant case there still remains much work to be done. You must read it, understand it, and analyze its potential relevance to the problem you are researching. This process may take more mental work than you have ever dedicated to just a few pages of text. It is not unusual for a lawyer to spend hours reading and re-reading a complex case. For a novice, this reading frequently involves referring to secondary sources for much needed background and context.

A. Analyzing the Substance of Cases

It can sometimes be difficult to determine whether a case is relevant to your research project. If the case concerns the same principles of law as the client's situation, the case is likely relevant. If the case also concerns the same legally significant facts as the client's situation, the case is almost certainly relevant. Legally significant facts are those that affect the court's decision. Some attorneys call these outcome-determinative facts or key facts. Which facts are legally significant depends upon the principle of law at issue.

Rarely will research reveal a case with facts that are exactly the same as a client's situation. Rather, several cases may involve facts that are similar to the client's situation but not exactly the same. An attorney's job is to determine whether the facts are similar enough for a court to apply the law in the same way and reach the same outcome. If the court reached a decision favorable to the client, the attorney will highlight the similarities. If, on the other hand, the court reached an unfavorable decision from the client's perspective, the attorney may argue that the case is distinguishable based on its facts or that its reasoning is faulty. Attorneys have an ethical duty to ensure that the court knows about a case directly on point, even if the outcome of that case is adverse to a client.

After determining that a case is relevant to some portion of a research project, you must decide how heavily it will weigh in your analysis. Two important points need to be considered here. One is the concept of *stare decisis*; the other is the difference between the holding of the case and dicta within that case.

Stare decisis means "to stand by things decided."[18] This means that courts must follow prior published opinions, ensuring consistency in the application of the law. This requirement, however, is limited to the courts within one jurisdiction. The Kansas Court of Appeals must follow the decisions of the Kansas Supreme Court, but not those of the courts of any other state. The concept of *stare decisis* also theoretically refers to a court with respect to its own opinions. However, for a variety of reasons, a court may sometimes decide not to continue following its earlier cases. Indeed, many of the most historically significant legal decisions involve a court overruling its prior precedent.[19]

---

18. *Black's Law Dictionary* 1442 (Bryan A. Garner, ed., 8th ed. West 2004).
19. *See generally Brown v. Bd. of Educ.*, 347 U.S. 483 (1954) (overruling *Plessy v. Ferguson*, 163 U.S. 537 (1896)).

Under *stare decisis*, courts are required to follow the holding of prior cases. The holding is the court's ultimate decision on the matter of law at issue in the case. Other statements or observations included in the opinion are not binding; they are referred to as *dicta*. In reaching its decision, the court may note that had the facts been slightly different, it would have decided the case differently. That observation is not binding on future courts, although its persuasive value should not be overlooked.

After finding a number of binding cases involving similar doctrine and facts, the next step is to synthesize the cases to state and explain the relevant legal rule. Sometimes a court states the rule fully; if not, piece together the information from the relevant cases to state the rule completely but concisely. Then use the analysis and facts of various cases to explain the law. Decide how the rule applies to the client's facts, and determine your conclusion. Note that this method of synthesis is much more than writing mere summaries of all the various cases. Legal analysis texts in Appendix B of this book explain synthesis in detail.

B. Strategies for Reading Cases

As you read cases, the following strategies may help you understand them more quickly and more thoroughly:

- Review the synopsis quickly to determine whether the case seems to be on point. If so, skim the headnotes to find the particular portion of the case that is relevant. Remember that one case may discuss several issue of law, only one or two of which may interest you. Go to the portion of the case identified by the relevant headnote and decide whether it is important for your project.

- If so, skim the entire case to get a feeling for what happened and why, focusing on the portion of the case identified by the relevant headnote.

- Read the case slowly and carefully. Skip the parts that are obviously not pertinent to your problem. For example, when researching a property question, there is no need to scrutinize the tort issue that is not pertinent to your property question.

- At the end of each paragraph or page, consider what you have read. If you cannot summarize it, try reading the material again.
- The next time you read the case, take notes. The notes may be in the form of a formal "case brief" or they may be scribbles that only you can understand. Regardless of the form, the process of taking notes will help you parse through, identify, and comprehend the essential concepts of the case. In law school, the notes will record your understanding of the case both for class discussion and for the end of the semester when you begin to review for exams. When preparing to write a legal document, the notes will assist you in organizing your analysis into an outline.
- Note that skimming text online or highlighting a printed page is often not sufficient to achieve thorough comprehension of judicial opinions.

Often you will read groups of cases as you conduct research. Reading the cases and understanding the law will be easier with an organized approach. First, organize groups of cases according to jurisdiction and then by date. Learning how the law developed over time in each jurisdiction will be easier if you read the cases chronologically. Finding the current rule of law will likely be easier if you begin with the most recent cases. Define your goal and organize the order in which you read the cases accordingly.

Pay attention to how the cases fit together. Look for trends in the law and in the facts of the cases. Has the law remained unchanged or have new elements been introduced? Has the meaning of an important term been redefined? Have certain facts virtually guaranteed success for one party while other facts have tended to cause difficulties? Does one case summarize the current rule or do you have to synthesize a rule from several cases that address part of the rule? All of these questions are crucial components of the legal analysis required for successful legal research.

Chapter 5

Digests

Chapter 4 described how cases are systematically published in chronological order. However, the cases are largely inaccessible because reporters do not organize cases by subject. Without a case finding aid, the legal researcher is seemingly buried under an avalanche of case law. Recognizing this dilemma, legal publishers long ago developed a remarkably effective way to index and classify published cases: digests.

A *digest* is a multi-volume index that organizes cases by subject. Under each subject, the digest provides a headnote from each case that addresses that particular subject. The scope of most digests is based on jurisdiction. There are separate digests for individual states, large geographic regions, and the entire federal court system.[1] These case finding aids have played such an important role in the United States common law system that every legal researcher needs a working knowledge of digests.

I. West Digests

Any discussion of digests necessarily involves the West Publishing Company.[2] To understand why, recall from Chapter 4 the important

---

1. Additional digests are covered in Part IV of this chapter.
2. Founded in 1872 by brothers John B. and Horatio West, the West Publishing Company merged with the Thomson Corporation in 1996. For an insightful look at the history of West, *see* Thomas A. Woxland, *"Forever Associated with the Practice of Law": The Early Years of the West Publishing Company*, 5(1) Leg. Ref. Servs. Q. 115 (1985).

contributions of West's *National Reporter System*. While the *National Reporter System* made the cases available chronologically, it did not make them readily accessible to the legal researcher. As a result, West's *American Digest System* was born.[3] The *American Digest System* organized the cases by subject and eventually became the industry standard for finding case law.

When you find cases using a digest, you are performing a skill with deep roots in legal tradition. Throughout most of the twentieth century, case law research almost always involved: 1) using the *American Digest System* to locate relevant cases, and 2) using the *National Reporter System* to read the full text of those cases. While this print-based paradigm is no longer the exclusive method of case finding, its continuing influence cannot be overstated. Mastering the print *American Digest System* will allow you to effectively use the newer electronic digest resources that have emerged. Furthermore, other publishers now offer their own digest systems, and the research patterns discussed here will generally translate to them as well.

A. Kansas Digests

The *American Digest System* consists of many separate digests that cover different jurisdictions. The state digest for Kansas is West's *Kansas Digest 2d*. Its coverage includes published cases from state and federal courts in Kansas. Published cases that originated in Kansas and were later decided by the United States Court of Appeals for the Tenth Circuit and the United States Supreme Court are also indexed in *Kansas Digest 2d*. The Tenth Circuit and U.S. Supreme Court coverage is therefore not comprehensive. To thoroughly examine federal case law, consult West's *Federal Practice Digest*, which indexes all published federal cases.

Kansas Digest 2d is not the only digest for Kansas. The regional digest for Kansas, West's *Pacific Digest*, is another viable option. *Kansas Digest 2d* and *Pacific Digest* offer largely overlapping, but not identi-

---

3. Actually, most of the system was purchased from Little, Brown. *Id.* at 120.

Table 5-1. Digest Coverage Summary

	Kansas Digest 2d	Pacific Digest	Federal Practice Digest
Kansas State Cases	✓	✓	✗
Other State Cases	✗	✓	✗
Kansas Federal Cases	✓	✗	✓
Other Federal Cases	✗	✗	✓
Cumulative	✓	✗	✗

cal, coverage. Both digests index all published Kansas state cases. *Pacific Digest*, however, has no federal court coverage. But it does offer something not found in *Kansas Digest 2d*: coverage of the other states represented in *Pacific Reporter*.[4] Taken together, *Pacific Reporter* and *Pacific Digest* report and index all published state cases in the Pacific region. Table 5-1 summarizes the coverage of *Kansas Digest 2d* and *Pacific Digest*. *Federal Practice Digest* is also included because sometimes you will need to research federal case law not contained in *Kansas Digest 2d* and *Pacific Digest*.

The "cumulative" category in Table 5-1 simply refers to the time frame covered by each digest. *Kansas Digest 2d* is cumulative, including cases decided since 1858, and replaces the original *Kansas Digest*. In contrast, *Pacific Digest* is not cumulative. Because *Pacific Digest* contains cases from fifteen states, it has been divided into different editions covering various time frames. Similarly, *Federal Practice Digest* is non-cumulative. Thus, several editions of these digests need to be consulted in order to comprehensively examine the evolution of a legal issue over the course of many decades. However, most of the time you will begin your research in the most recent edition and work backwards only when recent case law does not adequately resolve your legal question. The most recent edition of *Pacific Digest* includes cases

---

4. The Pacific region includes: Alaska, Arizona, California, Colorado, Hawaii, Idaho, Kansas, Montana, Nevada, New Mexico, Oklahoma, Oregon, Utah, Washington, and Wyoming.

decided since 1978, while the most recent edition of *Federal Practice Digest* includes cases decided since the mid-1980s.

B. Headnotes

To fully understand how digests and headnotes work, consider a case that has been successfully appealed to the Supreme Court of Kansas. When the Court publishes its decision, West's digest editors spring into action. They read and analyze the case, dissecting the opinion into its constituent parts. The digest editors take each legal issue addressed by the court and prepare a short summary, or abstract, for each one. These abstracts are called headnotes.

In reporters in the *National Reporter System*, headnotes appear before the official text of the court opinion. The headnotes serve an important shortcut function for the legal researcher. As noted in Chapter 4, headnotes are a shorthand version of a proposition of law. Skimming the headnotes allows you to quickly ascertain what legal issues are addressed in a case. Before each headnote there will be a number that corresponds with a portion of the official opinion.[5] If a particular headnote appears especially relevant, you can quickly locate the corresponding portion of the official opinion by means of the headnote number. It is important to read the official text of the court opinion because West's headnotes are not authoritative and should never be formally cited as legal authority.[6] Although research typically begins with skimming headnotes, before relying upon a case you must read the entire opinion to gain a complete understanding of its holding(s).

---

5. Be careful not to confuse headnote numbers with topic-key numbers.

6. While official *Kansas Reports*' "Syllabus by the Court" headnotes can be cited, they are not part of the *American Digest System* and therefore do not lead to similar cases. Furthermore, the official syllabus and text of the opinion is public domain while West's headnotes are proprietary and copyrighted by West.

C. Topics and Key Numbers

Headnotes do more than save you time reading the case; they provide the basis for West's digest system. West's editors classify each headnote with a *topic* and *key number* based upon the legal point that is the focus of the headnote. Topics and key numbers are the nuts and bolts of the *American Digest System*. Indeed, the *American Digest System* is often referred to as the "topic and key number system." The topic places the headnote within a broad subject area of the law. There are over four hundred major topics, all of which belong to one of West's "Seven Main Divisions of Law":

1) Persons
2) Property
3) Contracts
4) Torts
5) Crimes
6) Remedies
7) Government

Examples of West topics include "Bankruptcy," "Environmental Law," and "Sentencing and Punishment." After being assigned to a topic, the headnote is assigned a key number within that topic. The key number relates to a subtopic within that area of law. There are over 100,000 individual key numbers.[7] An example of a topic-key number for cases dealing with bankruptcy jurisdiction is "Bankruptcy 2041(1)." The key number 2041(1) refers to the subtopic "Bankruptcy jurisdiction-In general."

After the headnotes have been classified with topics and key numbers, they are separated and placed in the appropriate digest volumes. When the digests are updated, headnotes from the case will appear under their corresponding topics and key numbers. In essence, the case is chopped up into pieces and each piece is exported to its proper

---

7. For a detailed explanation of the topic and key number classification process, see *West's Analysis of American Law: Guide to the American Digest System* (Thomson/West 2006).

Figure 5-2. Excerpts from *Kansas Digest 2d* "Appeal & Error"

Kan. 1905. The certificate of the trial judge that the action involves the tax law of the state, thus giving the Supreme Court jurisdiction, is not binding on the latter.

Huffman v. Ackarman, 81 P. 168, 71 Kan. 873.

Kan.App. 2005. The Court of Appeals has a duty to question jurisdiction on its own initiative and dismiss an appeal if the record reveals a lack of jurisdiction.

In re D.I.G., 114 P.3d 173, 34 Kan.App.2d 34.

Source: *Kansas Digest 2d*. Reprinted with permission of Thomson Reuters/West.

home in the *American Digest System*. A published Kansas case's headnotes will be included in both *Kansas Digest 2d* and *Pacific Digest*, but the headnotes will always be classified the same way regardless of which West digest is consulted because the topic and key number system is uniform across all West digests.

In *Kansas Digest 2d*, headnotes are grouped by court under each topic-key number. Federal cases are listed first, followed by state court cases. Within the federal and state systems, cases are listed according to judicial hierarchy: cases from the highest appellate court are listed first, followed by decisions of intermediate appellate courts, then trial court cases. Cases from each court are given in reverse chronological order, allowing you to see the most recent cases first. Figure 5-2 illustrates the headnotes in *Kansas Digest 2d*.

At the beginning of each headnote is a court abbreviation and date. The abbreviations are explained in tables at the beginning of each digest volume. Some of the court abbreviations used in *Kansas Digest 2d* headnotes are listed in Table 5-3. Note the abbreviations are listed in the hierarchy used by *Kansas Digest 2d*.

Although West may have assigned a topic-key number to a particular point of law, a given jurisdiction may not have decided a case on that point. In that instance, no entries will appear under the topic-key number of that jurisdiction's digest. However, the topic-key number system makes it easy to research cases in other jurisdictions using

Table 5-3. Court Abbreviations in *Kansas Digest 2d*

U.S.Kan. 1990	A 1990 case that originated in Kansas and was decided by the United States Supreme Court
C.A.10 (Kan.) 2001	A 2001 case that originated in Kansas and was decided by the Tenth Circuit Court of Appeals
D.Kan. 1999	A 1999 case decided by the U.S. District Court for the District of Kansas
Kan. 2003	A 2003 case decided by the Supreme Court of Kansas
Kan.App. 2004	A 2004 case decided by the Kansas Court of Appeals

West digests, which may lead to persuasive authorities. For researching a Kansas issue with existing state or federal precedent, *Kansas Digest 2d* would probably be the best choice among digests. For researching a Kansas issue without existing state or federal precedent, *Pacific Digest* would probably be preferable because it might contain persuasive authority from other jurisdictions. The critical point is that, while the law may vary from jurisdiction to jurisdiction, its subject classification within the key number system does not.

II. Digest Research

Using digests is not a mechanical process. There is no predetermined starting or ending point. Rather, digest research offers several different entry points and stopping points. The research process typically involves a "feedback loop" between the digests and the reporters. You will find relevant cases in the digest, read them in the case reporter, return to the digest with a better understanding of your issue, locate more relevant cases, and repeat this process until your legal question is resolved.[8] The theme here is that digest research is not linear — it is cyclical.[9]

---

8. Remember that case law might not entirely resolve your legal question — other sources of primary law may also need to be consulted.

9. Note that, when researching Kansas state law in print, only the *Pacific Reporter* provides quick feedback between reporter and digest. This is be-

Table 5-4. Beginning with a Relevant Case

---

1) Find and read the relevant case (*see* Secondary Sources below in Section II.A.1.).
2) Identify the points of law that are relevant to your issue.
3) Identify the headnotes that correspond with those points of law.
4) Record the topic-key number classification for each headnote.
5) Examine those topic-key numbers in the appropriate digest.
6) Update your research (*see* Updating Your Research below in Section II.A.2.).
7) Record the citations for relevant cases identified in the digest.
8) Examine those cases in the appropriate case reporters.
9) Follow this feedback loop between the reporters and the digests until your legal question is resolved, consulting the Topic Analysis and Descriptive Word Index as needed.

There are three primary ways to launch your digest research process: 1) beginning with a relevant case, 2) beginning with the Topic Analysis, and 3) beginning with the Descriptive Word Index. The approach utilized will depend on the information you have when you begin your research and what you need to find.

A. Beginning with a Relevant Case

With a relevant case in hand, you can take a shortcut directly into the digest system. Table 5-4 summarizes the research process when you begin with a relevant case.

As noted in Table 5-4, even when beginning your research with a relevant case, it is a good idea to investigate the Topic Analysis feature (discussed below in Section II.B.) and the Descriptive Word Index (discussed below in Section II.C.) to ensure no relevant material is overlooked. While the research process described in Table 5-4

---

cause the *Pacific Reporter* includes West headnotes while *Kansas Reports* and *Kansas Court of Appeals Reports* do not.

may initially seem daunting, with practice each step becomes intuitive. Some of the more intricate steps are described below.

1. Secondary Sources

The preceding discussion begs the question, how do you find a relevant case in the first place? The primary answer, of course, is secondary sources.[10] Secondary sources such as treatises, legal encyclopedias, law review articles, and *American Law Reports* (*ALR*) annotations are replete with references to case law. Recall from Chapter 1 that the consultation of secondary sources typically occurs early in the research process. Digest research is no exception.

Consulting secondary sources first can provide easy access into the digest system because, in addition to case references, they offer an overview of the language and terms of art associated with a particular area of law. They will provide context and familiarity with the "big picture," which can only help when you are navigating the digest system. The bottom line is: consult secondary sources first, gain familiarity with your issue, and try to enter the digest system with a relevant case in hand. Making this method a habit will save you many hours of research time. See Chapter 3 for a detailed discussion of secondary sources and how to use them.

2. Updating Your Research

Legal research using print resources always involves updating your research. As with all print resources, the digest you are using is only as current as the volume's publication date. Table 5-5 summarizes the publications you should check when updating your digest research. This updating process applies to all print digest research, whether you are beginning with a relevant case, the Topical Analysis, or the Descriptive Word Index.

---

10. There are also many variations on this theme. For example, a reference from a supervising attorney, or a case reference in an annotated statutory code, are also potential avenues for obtaining an initial relevant case.

Table 5-5. Resources for Updating Digest Research

1) The main digest volumes
2) Either the pocket part or the volume supplement
3) The cumulative supplementary pamphlet
4) The reporters and advance sheets
5) The *General Digest*
6) Westlaw

Legal publishers periodically update the bound volumes with paperback pocket parts and supplements. *Kansas Digest 2d* and *Pacific Digest* are updated with pocket parts once a year (or a soft-cover volume supplement if the updated information is too thick to fit into a pocket part), along with a *cumulative supplementary pamphlet* twice a year. Cumulative supplementary pamphlets contain updates for all topics and are typically shelved after all the volumes in the digest. You must always remember to check all relevant pocket parts and supplements, lest you miss an important recent development in the law.

Finally, you must confront the fact that the pocket parts and supplements are often a few months old. This means there is a time-gap between your research and the present. You must find a way to fill in that time-gap because the courts have undoubtedly continued to publish opinions, some of which might be relevant to your issue. Luckily, the *National Reporter System* offers a solution to this problem. Go to *Pacific Reporter*'s most recent volumes and advance sheets and locate the "mini-digest" contained in each. It will appear near the beginning of the volume and is entitled *Key Number Digest*. That a tiny piece of the digest system is actually found in case reporters illustrates the interlocking nature of the *National Reporter System* and the *American Digest System*—they are meant to be used together. [11]

---

11. A table at the beginning of each digest volume will indicate which reporter volumes are indexed there. Updating requires you to check the digest sections of subsequent reporters.

Table 5-6. Beginning with the Topic Analysis

---

1) Examine the Topic Analysis for relevant key numbers.
2) Examine those key numbers for relevant headnotes.
3) Update your research (*see* Updating Your Research in Section II.A.2.).
4) Record the citations for relevant cases identified in the digest.
5) Examine those cases in the appropriate case reporters.
6) Follow this feedback loop between the reporters and the digests until your legal question is resolved, consulting the Topic Analysis and Descriptive Word Index as needed.

The *General Digest*, which is a component of the comprehensive *Decennial Digest* system discussed in Section IV.A., offers yet another updating feature. Consulting the most recent *General Digest* volumes can bring your research very close to the present. Of course, there will always be another window of time after advance sheet and *General Digest* publication. For same day currency, you must go to an online database — in this case, Westlaw. Again, this updating process applies to all print digest research, whether beginning with a relevant case, the Topic Analysis, or the Descriptive Word Index.

B. Beginning with the Topic Analysis

If you are familiar with the general area of law implicated by your research problem (and how it is classified in the *American Digest System*), you can begin your research using the Analysis outline that appears at the beginning of each relevant topic. Table 5-6 summarizes the research process when you begin with the Topic Analysis.

Scanning the list of key number subtopics and reviewing the corresponding headnotes can quickly lead to relevant cases. Longer topics will contain a short, summary outline and then a detailed outline. Many topics follow a general litigation organization, so that elements,

Figure 5-7. Excerpts from *Kansas Digest 2d* Analysis
for "Appeal & Error"

Analysis

I. NATURE AND FORM OF REMEDY, ☞ 1–16.
II. NATURE AND GROUNDS OF APPELLATE JURISDICTION, ☞ 17–23.
III. DECISIONS REVIEWABLE, ☞ 24–135.

    (A) COURTS AND OTHER TRIBUNALS SUBJECT TO
        REVIEW, ☞ 24–32.

    (B) NATURE OF SUBJECT-MATTER AND CHARACTER OF
        PARTIES, ☞ 33–44.

    (C) AMOUNT OR VALUE IN CONTROVERSY, ☞ 45–65.

    (D) FINALITY OF DETERMINATION, ☞ 66–84.

Source: *Kansas Digest 2d*. Reprinted with permission of Thomson Reuters/
West.

defenses, pleadings, and evidence are discussed in that order. Figure
5-7 provides an example of the Analysis feature.

As always, don't forget to update your research. Remember to
check the pocket parts (or volume supplements), cumulative supplementary pamphlets, reporter advance sheets, the *General Digest*, and
Westlaw for more recent cases under the topics and key numbers you
are investigating. Finally, even when beginning research with the
Topic Analysis, it is a good idea to consult the Descriptive Word Index
to ensure no relevant material is overlooked.

C. Beginning with the Descriptive Word Index

Suppose you do not have a relevant case and you are not familiar
with the area of law implicated by your legal question.[12] In this situ-

---

12. Ideally, you should consult secondary sources in this situation. There
may be times, however, when you do not have access to a relevant secondary
source.

Table 5-8. Beginning with the Descriptive Word Index

1) Develop a list of research terms.
2) Find the research terms in the Descriptive Word Index, which will list topics and key numbers relevant to those terms.
3) Update the Descriptive Word Index with pocket parts and the *General Digest.*
4) Review each topic-key number in the main volumes of the digest.
5) Update each topic-key number by checking the pocket parts or volume supplement, the cumulative supplementary pamphlets, reporters and advance sheets, the *General Digest*, and Westlaw.
6) Read all of the relevant cases that your research reveals in the appropriate case reporters.
7) Follow this feedback loop between the reporters and digests until your legal question is resolved, consulting the Topic Analysis and Descriptive Word Index as needed.

ation, the Descriptive Word Index is the best entry point into the digest system. The traditional importance of using the Descriptive Word Index makes this process a staple of most legal research courses.

Located near the end of a digest set, the Descriptive Word Index is essentially an index for an index: the digest indexes the *National Reporter System*, and the Descriptive Word Index indexes the digest. As West describes the Descriptive Word Index, it is "[u]nique in that it indexes both facts and law, it is the master key which enables the busy lawyer to unlock the door to decisional law involving factual situations and legal principles similar to those involved in the problem before him."[13] Table 5-8 provides an outline of the Descriptive Word Index research process.

1. Developing a List of Research Terms

Follow the TARPP or journalistic brainstorming method from Chapter 1, or use your own approach to generate a list of research

13. This language appears in the preface to West digest Descriptive Word Index volumes.

terms that describe the situation you are analyzing. Don't forget that secondary sources often provide an introduction to the language and terms of art associated with an area of law. In addition, West advises the researcher to consider the "five elements common to every case: 1) The **Parties** involved; 2) The **Places** where the facts arose, and the **Objects** or **Things** involved; 3) The **Acts** or **Omissions** which form the **Basis of Action** or **Issue**; 4) The **Defense** to the action or issue; and 5) The **Relief** sought."[14]

2. Finding the Research Terms in the Descriptive Word Index

Look up each of your research terms and record the topic-key number for each term you find. Some topics are abbreviated in the Descriptive Word Index. A list of topics and their abbreviations is included at the front of each index volume. Figure 5-9 shows an excerpt from the Descriptive Word Index in *Kansas Digest 2d*.

Finding research terms in the Descriptive Word Index is not always easy, especially if you are not familiar with an area of law. Using the Descriptive Word Index efficiently takes some practice and can be a deceptively time-consuming task. The process will eventually become less labor-intensive as you gain familiarity with its structure. Above all else, take a flexible approach when locating research terms in the Descriptive Word Index. Rarely will your first guess lead directly to relevant cases, or even an index entry for that matter. There will be dead ends and false leads along the way, but a little persistence can usually reveal a relevant topic. In sum, be prepared to exercise your vocabulary when using the Descriptive Word Index.

3. Updating the Descriptive Word Index

Much like the main digest volumes, the Descriptive Word Index is updated with pocket parts. To be thorough, you must search these pocket parts for each of your research terms and record any topics

---

14. This language appears in the preface to West digest Descriptive Word Index volumes (emphasis in original).

Figure 5-9. Excerpts from the Descriptive Word Index
in *Kansas Digest 2d*

CONTRACTS   32 Kan D 2d-164

References are to Digest Topics and Key Numbers

CONTRACTS – Cont'd

CONFIDENTIAL information, contracts
  preventing disclosure of, **Contracts** 🔑 118

CONFLICT of laws. See heading
  CONFLICT OF LAWS, CONTRACTS.

CONFLICTING clauses, **Contracts** 🔑 162

CONSENT judgments or orders, **Fed Civ**
  Proc 2397; **Judgm** 🔑 71.1

CONSIDERATION,
  Generally, **Contracts** 🔑 47–91

Source: *Kansas Digest 2d*. Reprinted with permission of Thomson Reuters/West.

and key numbers you find. The *General Digest* also offers updated Descriptive Word Index entries. Check the most recent *General Digest* volumes to cover any remaining time-gaps.

4. Reviewing Each Topic-Key Number in the Main Volumes of the Digest

After consulting the Descriptive Word Index, you should be armed with several potentially relevant topics and key numbers. You are now ready to begin examining the digest entries for these topics and key numbers, searching for relevant headnotes. The relevant headnotes you find in the digest will lead you to the relevant cases that are "hidden" in the reporters.

Kansas Digest 2d and *Pacific Digest* are organized according to West's 400 topics in alphabetical order. Select the volume containing your first potential topic, noting that not all topics are listed on the spine of each volume. For example, in the current *Kansas Digest 2d*, the topic "Antitrust & Trade Regulation" is included in the volume "Animals to Appeal & Error." Sometimes one topic will span more than one digest volume.

After locating the appropriate digest volume, locate the page where the entry for your topic begins. At the beginning of each topic you will find the "Subjects Included" feature. Examine this list for subjects that are potentially relevant to your research issue. Next, examine the "Subjects Excluded and Covered by Other Topics" feature. Be sure to make a note of any promising research leads you find here. The Topic Analysis, discussed above in Section II.B., follows these lists. Even with relevant key numbers in hand, it is a good idea to skim the Topic Analysis and see where the key numbers fit within the structure of the topic. Moreover, skimming the Topic Analysis may reveal new key numbers that are relevant to your issue.

You are now ready to begin reading headnotes. Like using the Descriptive Word Index, skimming headnotes is a skill that must be cultivated with practice. The sometimes rambling and abstract translations are not always easy to read, and often a wide variation of holdings will be grouped under one key number. However, after reading several headnotes under a key number you will see some patterns begin to emerge because comparing the headnotes to each other provides some context. There might not be a headnote that is directly on point with your inquiry; however, juxtaposing the different holdings may yield some relevant rules of law. Note the case citation for any headnotes that appear relevant to your inquiry.

5. Updating Each Topic-Key Number

As always, you must update each topic-key number with pocket parts, supplements, advance sheets, the *General Digest*, and Westlaw. Revisit the discussion in Section II.A.2. for an in-depth discussion of this process.

6. Reading the Relevant Cases that Your Research Reveals

After identifying potentially relevant cases in the digest, read those cases in the appropriate case reporters. When you go to the reporters and locate your first case, quickly skim the synopsis to see whether the case appears to be on point. Next, find each relevant headnote and turn to that part of the case. Remember, the number in brackets before each headnote corresponds with a passage of the official text of the court opinion. Find the corresponding number in brackets within the official text. Skim that portion of the case. Only when you have skimmed the relevant parts of a case should you consider photocopying, printing, or taking notes from it. Do not waste paper, money, or your time by delaying the difficult work of analyzing cases. Furthermore, later in the research process you will need to carefully read the entire case to ensure complete comprehension of its holdings. At this point, however, skimming is typically adequate for narrowing down the list of relevant cases.

7. Following the Feedback Loop

Your research process will rarely end with one consultation of the digest and one trip to the case reporters. Rather, the cases you read in the reporters will raise new issues. These issues might be classified under new topic-key numbers. Thus, you will return to the digest and examine those topic-key numbers.

Remember that only West case reporters will provide headnotes classified in the *American Digest System*. For example, *Pacific Reporter* is part of the *National Reporter System* and provides West headnotes with topic-key numbers that can be examined in either *Kansas Digest 2d* or *Pacific Reporter*. However, *Kansas Reports* and *Kansas Court of Appeals Reports* are not part of the *National Reporter System* and do not include West headnotes. Accordingly, if you begin with the official copy of a case, look up the parallel cite and find the *Pacific Reporter* copy because the headnotes and topic-key numbers offer a considerable research advantage.

D. Digest Research Summary

Section II reviewed three of the primary ways to perform digest research: 1) beginning with a case, 2) beginning with the Topic Analy-

Table 5-10. Digest Research Summary

Initial Information	Best Research Strategy
A relevant published case with West headnotes	Beginning with a relevant case
Familiarity with the general area of law and where it is classified in the *American Digest System* (but no relevant case citation)	Beginning with the Topic Analysis
Very little initial information, perhaps some terms of art	Beginning with the Descriptive Word Index

sis, and 3) beginning with the Descriptive Word Index. While each of these strategies begins in a different place, digest research will often overlap among the three. Mastery of all three methods is necessary to realize the full potential of this case-finding aid. Deciding where to begin digest research is largely a function of how much information you initially have. Table 5-10 summarizes the different entry points into the digest system.

III. Other Useful Digest Features

The preceding section discussed the most common methods of locating cases using a digest. However, several other useful digest features can make the researcher's task much easier.

A. Words and Phrases

When seeking the definition of a legal term, the common first step is to consult *Black's Law Dictionary*. However, sometimes you will need to know more than the general definition — you will need to know how a particular court has interpreted it. For example, courts often add a "judicial gloss" to the meaning of vague statutory terms.

A digest feature called Words and Phrases lists cases that define the term in question. *Kansas Digest 2d* and *Pacific Digest* offer Words and Phrases volumes located toward the end of the digest set. The Words and Phrases volumes basically function as a mini-digest that is focused exclusively upon the definition of legal terms.

Terms are listed in Words and Phrases alphabetically, followed by references to cases that define each term. Each reference includes the full name and citation of the case as well as a short description of the case. At the end of each entry in the Words and Phrases volumes, West lists the topics and key numbers used for that case's headnotes. The information in Words and Phrases volumes is updated with pocket parts and reporter advance sheets. West also publishes a comprehensive multi-jurisdictional series entitled *Words and Phrases*.

B. Table of Cases

The Table of Cases lists all the cases indexed in a particular digest series by both the primary plaintiff's name and the primary defendant's name. This table is helpful when you do not know the citation to a relevant case. This often occurs when a colleague recommends the case or you have used it in previous research but cannot recall the exact citation. The Table of Cases provides the full name of the case, the citation for the case, and the relevant topics and key numbers. After consulting the Table of Cases, you could either read the case in a reporter or continue working in the digest using the topics and key numbers to find more related cases.

IV. Other Digest Systems

While this chapter has focused on West digests that are particularly useful for legal research in Kansas, you may encounter many other digests in your research. For example, in addition to digests based on jurisdiction, West also publishes topical digests such as *Bankruptcy Digest* and *Military Justice Digest*.

All digests that are part of West's *American Digest System* work the same way. There are also non-West digest systems that, although they do not employ the *American Digest System*'s topic and key number scheme, will largely function in the same way.

A. *Decennial Digest*

West's *Decennial Digest* indexes cases from all United States jurisdictions that are reported in the *National Reporter System*. The headnotes listed under each entry are arranged by jurisdiction and date. You may find the *Decennial Digest* helpful in the following circumstances:

- Your library does not contain a digest for the jurisdiction you are researching.
- There is no law on point in your jurisdiction, requiring you to search the laws of other jurisdictions for persuasive authority.

The *Decennial Digest* used to be published every ten years, hence its name, but it is now published in two parts, each part covering a five-year period. *Decennial Digests* are updated with the *General Digest*. To search the *Decennial Digest* thoroughly, you must look in each series containing cases from the period relevant for your project. For the most recent cases, check the *General Digest* volumes.

B. Supreme Court Digests

Although *Federal Practice Digest* offers comprehensive federal court coverage, sometimes your research may be squarely focused on United States Supreme Court cases. In such instances, a Supreme Court digest may be especially helpful. West publishes *United States Supreme Court Digest* as part of the *American Digest System*. Accordingly, research using this resource largely tracks the general research strategies discussed in this chapter.

West is not the only publisher of a Supreme Court digest. Indeed, LexisNexis publishes the *United States Supreme Court Digest, Lawyers' Edition*. Originally published by Lawyers Cooperative Publishing, this resource represents perhaps the most historically entrenched competition for the print *American Digest System*. Regardless of which resource you use, remember that they are distinct digest systems that must be used separately. For example, you cannot use a West topic-key number to find a case in the *Lawyers' Edition* digests.

C. Electronic Digests

Both Westlaw and LexisNexis provide online digests. Westlaw offers an electronic version of the *American Digest System*. *Lawyers' Edition* headnotes now appear in LexisNexis electronic publications. However, LexisNexis has also developed another digest system that is not limited to Supreme Court opinions. Appearing only in electronic format, with no print counterpart, this system now competes with the topic and key number system available on Westlaw. Thus, Supreme Court cases viewed electronically on LexisNexis contain two sets of headnotes: 1) *Lawyers' Edition* headnotes, and 2) LexisNexis headnotes. All other cases viewed electronically on LexisNexis include only LexisNexis headnotes.

Online digest systems offer the best of both worlds: the comprehensive indexing of print digests *and* the speed and efficiency of electronic research. If you understand how to perform digest research using print materials, your knowledge will easily translate into an electronic environment. Chapter 11 explains the basics of online digest research.

Chapter 6

Updating with Citators

The law is a moving target. Legal authorities are continually being interpreted or modified in any number of ways. For example, as thousands of cases accumulate in libraries and databases, determining which cases to rely upon becomes increasingly difficult. An on-point case is little help if it is no longer "good law." The case's validity must be determined because subsequent litigation may have, among other things, reversed or overruled the case. Accordingly, authority cannot be viewed in a vacuum—it must be analyzed within the context of what follows it. Given the sheer volume of existing authority, this type of analysis poses a considerable challenge for the legal researcher. *Citators* are the tools that evolved to help researchers quickly "update" cases and determine their weight as precedent.

Although this chapter primarily focuses on cases, the process of updating is not limited to the judicial branch. Before using any legal authority to analyze a problem, a researcher must know how that authority has been treated by later actions of a court, legislature, or agency. For example, just as a case may have been reversed or overruled, a statute may have been amended or repealed. A wide range of authorities from both federal and state jurisdictions can be updated using citators, including constitutions, statutes, regulations and other administrative materials, patents, and secondary sources.

Updating an authority requires finding every subsequent legal source that has cited the authority and determining how the subsequent source treated that authority on a particular issue. The starting point for updating is obtaining a list of citations to sources that refer to the authority. Fortunately, the list need not be created from scratch. Citators, both print and electronic, have already created the list. Interpreting the results on the list will typically occupy most of the researcher's time, and legal research is not finished until this crucial step has been completed for each authority that will be used in a legal argument. |

Although electronic citators are rapidly supplanting print citators as the industry standard, this chapter begins with a discussion of the print publication *Shepard's Citations* due to its historical significance within the American legal system. Just as the story of digests cannot be told without reference to West's *American Digest System*, citators cannot be discussed without mentioning *Shepard's Citations*, or "Shepard's" for short. Furthermore, mastery of the updating process in print makes it easier to understand the information provided by electronic citators. This chapter then examines the electronic version of Shepard's (available on LexisNexis) and its primary competitor, KeyCite (found on Westlaw). The chapter concludes with some frequently asked questions, a discussion of how updating fits within the research landscape, and a brief note regarding the importance of updating within the context of legal ethics.

I. Updating in Print

Understanding the process of updating requires familiarity with two basic terms: the cited source and the citing sources. The authority you are updating is called the *cited source*. In this chapter a case is used as the cited source. The authorities listed in a citator that refer to that case are called *citing sources* or sometimes *citing references* or *citing decisions*. Although the terminology is very similar, just remember that there is only one cited source in each search while there may be many citing sources.

The process of updating includes finding all the subsequent sources that cite your case, analyzing the symbols provided by the citator, and reading the citing sources to determine their impact on your case. The process of updating with Shepard's in print is similar to updating online with one important exception: the citing references are contained in multiple volumes rather than in one electronic

Table 6-1. Outline for Shepardizing in Print

1. Review the cover of the most recent Shepard's pamphlet for a chart called "What Your Library Should Contain." Gather the relevant Shepard's volumes and supplements listed in that chart.
2. Compile lists of citing references. Analyze the citations and Shepard's analytical symbols.
3. Prioritize and read the citing references. Analyze the impact, if any, the authorities have on the source you are updating.

list. The cumbersome process of gathering the correct volumes may seem arcane to the electronic generation, but before the advent of electronic researching print Shepard's was *the way* authority was updated. Indeed, updating is still often generically referred to as "Shepardizing." Table 6-1 provides an outline for Shepardizing in print.

The jurisdiction or the reporter where your case was published will indicate which Shepard's title you will need for updating. Lists of citations to Kansas cases are included in *Shepard's Kansas Citations* and *Shepard's Pacific Reporter Citations.*[1] Each Shepard's title includes multiple volumes and supplements.

A. Collect Relevant Shepard's Volumes

Shepard's volumes and supplements are not cumulative, so comprehensive Shepardizing in print requires finding lists of citations in several volumes and pamphlets to cover the time span from when a case was decided to the present.

On the cover of the most recent supplement[2] is a chart called "What Your Library Should Contain." Review that chart and collect

---

1. Shepardizing a Kansas case in the two citators may produce slightly different results because their coverage is slightly different. Tables at the front of each Shepard's volume state which citing sources are included.
2. If a supplement is more than one month old, there is likely a more recent supplement available for use. To determine whether a supplement is the most recent available, ask a law librarian.

the relevant volumes and supplements listed there.[3] Shepard's maroon volumes and supplements contain the most information, but they are soon outdated. These hardbound volumes are updated by soft-cover pamphlets with gold, red, white, or blue paper covers. The color indicates the period covered. Gold covers indicate annual or semiannual updates. Red covers indicate pamphlets with coverage over several months. White supplements, called *advance sheets*, generally cover just a few weeks. Some Shepard's series have blue *express supplements* that generally cover periods of a few weeks, too.

B. Compile Lists of Citations from Multiple Shepard's Volumes

Look up your citation in each of the relevant volumes and supplements.[4] The example in Figure 6-2 is for the case *Mendenhall v. Roberts*, 17 Kan. App. 2d 34 (1992). Each column represents the citations found in a separate volume or supplement. Note that, in the interest of space, Shepard's has devised its own abbreviation system. Referring to a table of abbreviations at the beginning of the Shepard's volumes is essential.

C. Analyze the Citations and Shepard's Symbols

The first few pages of any Shepard's volume or supplement will contain a sample list of citing sources, along with explanatory text. Review this material carefully to learn about the codes that Shepard's uses to indicate the way that the citing sources treat the case you are updating. For example, a letter preceding a citing source may show that the case you are updating has been overruled ("o"), reversed ("r"), distinguished ("d"), or followed ("f"). The following passage,

---

3. When updating a case, volumes with statutes as cited sources are not needed. Also, volumes published before the date of your case are unnecessary.

4. If you have just a party's name, use *Shepard's Kansas Case Names Citator* or the Table of Cases in *Kansas Digest 2d* to find the case's citation.

Figure 6-2. Excerpts from *Shepard's Kansas Citations*
for *Mendenhall v. Roberts,* 17 Kan. App. 2d 34 (1992)

1994 Bound Volume Case Edition, Part 2 (maroon bound)	1994–2001 Bound Supplement (maroon bound)	March 2007 Annual Cumulative Supplement (yellow pamphlet)
- 31 -	- 31 -	
Ottawa	19KA2d^{2}272	Vol. 17
v McMechan		
1992	- 34 -	- 11 -
(829P2d927)	21KA2d6	Cir. 10
	f 27KA2d734	f 2005Bankr LX
- 34 -	Cir. 10	[865
Mendenhall	39F3d1137	
v Roberts	820FS1341	- 34 -
1992	839FS779	272Kan557
(831P2d568)	839FS780	29KA2d571
17KA2d390		31KA2d982
Cir. 10	- 47 -	
820FS1341	d 254Kan811	- 59 -
41KLR672		275Kan120
	- 59 -	275Kan^{4}615
- 47 -	d 1999KanApp	275Kan^{3}616
In the Matter	[LX1536	28KA2d^{5}338
of the Marriage	1999KanApp	d 28KA2d339
of Thompson	[LX^{5}1536	
1992	h 20KA2d290	
(832P2d349)		

Sources: *Shepard's Kansas Citations, 1994 Bound Volume, Case Edition, Part 2*, page 616; *1994–2001 Bound Supplement*, page 200; *Annual Cumulative Supplement, Vol. 79 No. 3*, page 160. Copyright 2008 LexisNexis, a division of Reed Elsevier Inc. All Rights Reserved.

written by a highly regarded legal research scholar, illustrates the learning curve associated with this process:

> Generations of law students suffered through mental torture trying to fathom what Shepard's was telling them. Sometimes when I taught legal research to law students I would snap open a volume of Shepard's, with its long lists of numbers and alphanumerics, let the students gasp, and then in-

tone, "These are the enchanted books of legal research. You will learn to be sorcerers."[5]

In print Shepardizing, the *headnote reference* is a small superscript number that appears between the reporter abbreviation and the page number. This number relates to a specific headnote from the case you are updating, not from the citing source, and allows you to quickly identify cases that address a specific legal issue. This feature was discontinued in 2006, although it remains quite useful for cases decided prior to 2006. Keep in mind that these headnote references will be keyed to a certain case reporter and will not be helpful unless you are utilizing the appropriate reporter.[6]

The first Shepard's entry for a cited source will offer "history" references to other documents that are part of the same litigation. These references are denoted with an "s." "Treatment" cases (subsequent citing cases) follow, and they are arranged by jurisdiction, beginning with the jurisdiction of the case being updated. Within that jurisdiction, cases are listed by court hierarchy and then in chronological order. Following cases, other sources that cite your case may be listed, such as law review articles or *American Law Reports (ALR)*.

Use the citations in Shepard's to find the full text of the citing sources. As you read the citing sources, decide whether they address the legal issue in your client's problem. If a source analyzes only points of your case that are not relevant to your client's situation, disregard that source. If a source is on point, analyze its impact on your case: Does this new source change the rule announced in your case, either by reversing or overruling it? Or does it follow your case by simply restating the rule and applying it to a similar fact pattern? Does the new source distinguish or criticize your case? If so, why and how? Be wary of unfavorable criticism of your authorities—opposing counsel will be quick to point it out to the judge.

---

5. Robert C. Berring, *Legal Information and the Search for Cognitive Authority*, 88 Cal. L. Rev. 1673, 1699 (2000).

6. For example, *Shepard's Citations* in print previously offered headnote references corresponding with the West topic and key number system. The electronic version of Shepard's now utilizes LexisNexis headnotes.

Table 6-3. Outline for Updating Online

1. Access the citator and enter your citation in the box provided.
2. Select the type of citation list you need: a short list showing the direct history and negative treatment of the cited source, or a longer list showing all subsequent citing sources.
3. Review the analytical symbols provided by the citator. Consider limiting the list of citing references by jurisdiction, headnote, date, or other function.
4. Prioritize and read the citing sources. Analyze the impact, if any, these sources have on the authority being updated. (This last step is identical to updating using print Shepard's.)

II. Updating Online

After using the time-honored but unwieldy print Shepard's volumes, one can truly appreciate the benefits of online citators. These electronic resources provide the most efficient way to update authorities, especially when the researcher understands their print-paradigm roots. The process of updating with an online citator is summarized in Table 6-3.

The electronic version of Shepard's is available on LexisNexis; Westlaw provides a competing service called "KeyCite." KeyCite is only available electronically—West does not publish print KeyCite volumes. Using these services to compile a list of citations is quite easy; for each service, simply type a citation in the appropriate box and run the search. Alternatively, online citators can be accessed when viewing the text of a case by clicking on the citator symbol at the top of the case. Understanding the search results can be tedious at first, although some features make it less difficult in comparison to print Shepard's. Updating, whether print or electronic, becomes second-nature with practice.

A. Shepard's on LexisNexis

Currently, Kansas's cases, statutes, constitution, court rules (but not administrative rules), attorney general opinions, and law review and bar journals can be Shepardized. From the "Shepard's" screen, click on "Citation Formats" for a list of publications covered. The list is likely to expand, so checking occasionally for new additions is a good research habit to adopt.

1. Access the Citator

You may access Shepard's from two points on LexisNexis. If you are already viewing a document, click on the "Shepardize" link at the top of the page. Otherwise, click on the "Shepard's" tab from the "Research" screen. Type the citation into the box. (If you need help with the format used by Shepard's, click on the "Citation Formats" link to the right of the box.)

2. Select the Type of Citing List

To determine which list of citing sources you retrieve, select one of the radio buttons. "Shepard's for Validation" will provide a limited list of citing sources, intended to show only whether your case is still good law. To obtain a complete list of citing sources, click on "Shepard's for Research."

3. Analyze the Citator Symbols and Limit the Search Results

The top of the results page has a symbol that indicates Shepard's opinion of the effect subsequent authorities have had on the validity of your cited source. To learn what a particular symbol means, rest your cursor over the symbol. For a full list of symbols and their meanings, scroll down to the legend provided at the bottom of any Shepard's result screen. A partial list of symbols is provided in Table 6-4. Remember that the symbols are only preliminary indicators and do not relieve you of the burden of reading significant citing sources and determining for yourself the continued validity of your case.

The Shepard's screen on LexisNexis begins with a summary of results; often this summary is in a grey box. Clicking on a term will allow you to skip through the search results to each citing source that

Table 6-4. Selected Symbols for Updating Cases
with Shepard's and KeyCite

KeyCite Symbol	Shepard's Symbol	Meaning
Red flag	Red stop sign	Negative treatment; the case may no longer be good law
Yellow flag	Yellow triangle	Possible negative treatment, though less strong than a red symbol
Green "C"	Green diamond	Positive treatment
Blue "H"	Blue "A" or "I"	Citing sources are available

treats your case in that way.[7] To go to the cases that follow your authority, for example, click on "Followed" in the summary box. Figure 6-5 shows the first screen of the *Mendenhall* case, using Shepard's for Research.

Each citing source is shown with its own Shepard's symbol at the end of the source's citation in the Shepard's results list. Clicking the hyperlinked name of the citing source will take you to that source, as will clicking one of the pinpoint citations listed below the case name. Clicking on the Shepard's symbol at the end of the source's citation will take you to the Shepard's list for that source. Remember not to confuse these symbols with the symbol for the case you are updating. The more useful symbol is the one at the top of the page that gives the Shepard's view of your case.

The search results can be filtered by type of analysis, key words, jurisdiction, date, and headnote.[8] This feature in Shepard's is called "FOCUS-Restrict By" and is provided via a link at the top of any Shep-

---

7. Some browsers do not support this function. An alternative is to use the "Find" function on your computer.

8. The headnotes will typically correspond to the LexisNexis headnote system.

Figure 6-5. Shepard's for Research

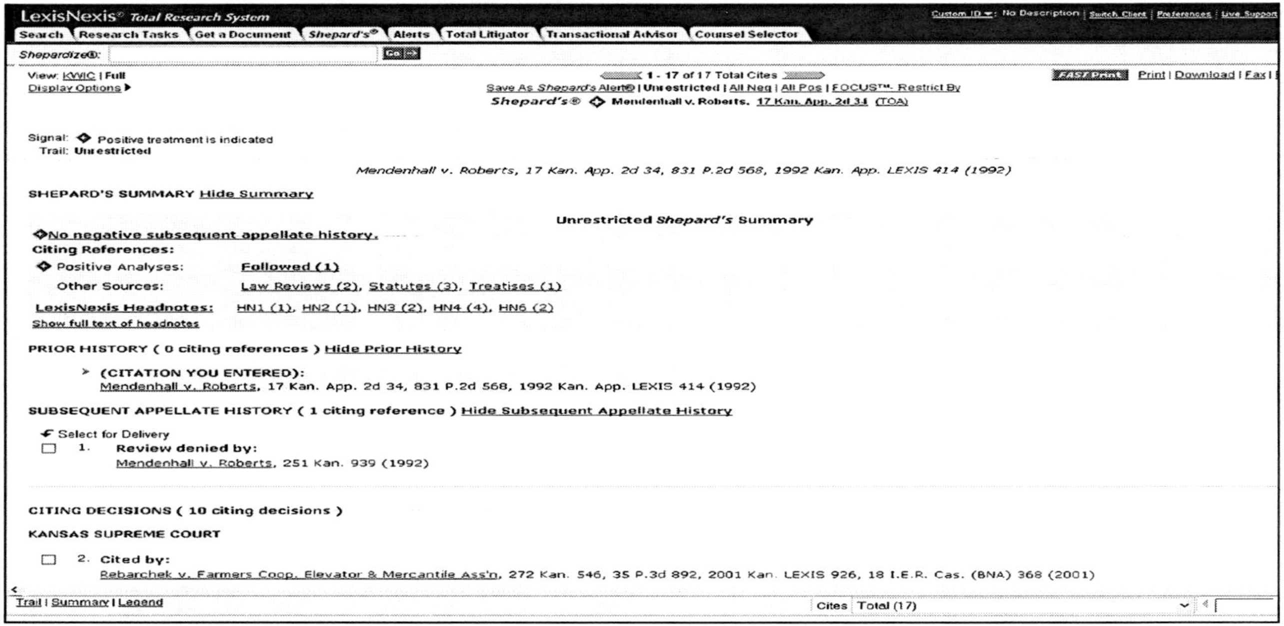

Source: LexisNexis. Copyright 2008 LexisNexis, a division of Reed Elsevier Inc. All Rights Reserved. LexisNexis and the Knowl-edge Burst logo are registered trademarks of Reed Elsevier Properties Inc. and are used with the permission of LexisNexis.

Figure 6-6. LexisNexis Restrictions

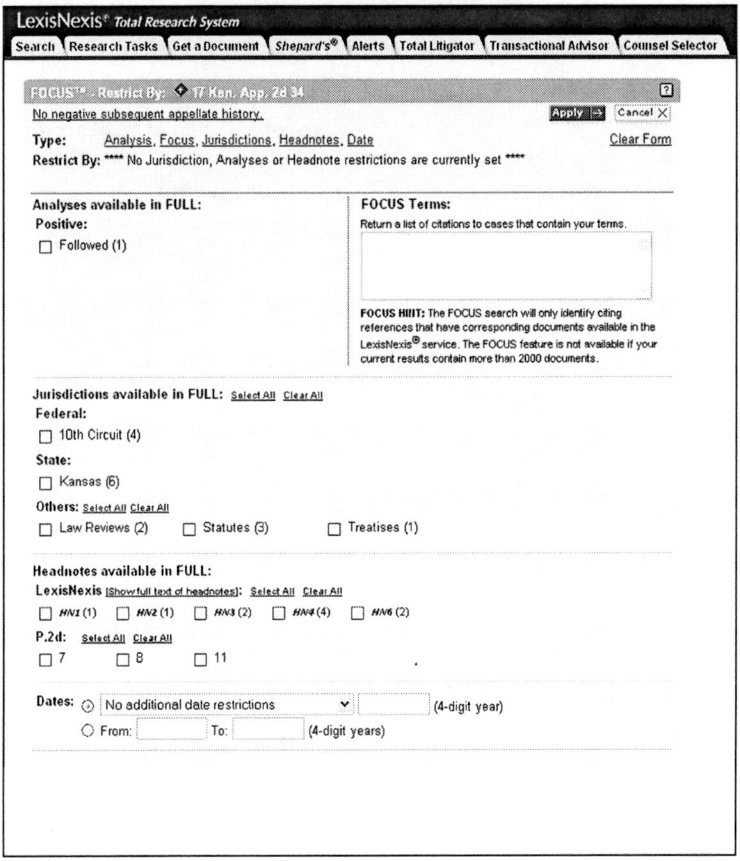

LexisNexis® *Total Research System*

Search ＼ Research Tasks ＼ Get a Document ＼ *Shepard's*® ＼ Alerts ＼ Total Litigator ＼ Transactional Advisor ＼ Counsel Selector

FOCUS™ - Restrict By: ◆ 17 Kan. App. 2d 34

No negative subsequent appellate history.

Apply ⇒ Cancel ✕

Type:　　Analysis, Focus, Jurisdictions, Headnotes, Date

Restrict By: **** No Jurisdiction, Analyses or Headnote restrictions are currently set ****

Clear Form

Analyses available in FULL:
Positive:
☐ Followed (1)

FOCUS Terms:
Return a list of citations to cases that contain your terms.

FOCUS HINT: The FOCUS search will only identify citing references that have corresponding documents available in the LexisNexis® service. The FOCUS feature is not available if your current results contain more than 2000 documents.

Jurisdictions available in FULL: Select All　Clear All
Federal:
☐ 10th Circuit (4)
State:
☐ Kansas (6)
Others: Select All　Clear All
☐ Law Reviews (2)　　☐ Statutes (3)　　☐ Treatises (1)

Headnotes available in FULL:
LexisNexis [Show full text of headnotes]:　Select All　Clear All
☐ HN1 (1)　☐ HN2 (1)　☐ HN3 (2)　☐ HN4 (4)　☐ HN6 (2)
P.2d:　Select All　Clear All
☐ 7　　　☐ 8　　　☐ 11

Dates: ⊙ No additional date restrictions ∨ ＿＿＿ (4-digit year)
　　　　 ○ From: ＿＿＿　To: ＿＿＿　(4-digit years)

ard's page. Follow that link to see all of your filtering options. Figure 6-6 shows the options available for the *Mendenhall* case. Simply click on the desired options, and leave the rest blank. In addition, a search box allows you to restrict your Shepard's search by terms. When you have selected the options and added any restrictive terms, click the "Apply" button. A filtered list of Shepard's results will be displayed.

4. Read and Analyze the Citing Sources

Again, the most important part of updating is reading the citing sources and deciding the impact they have on your authority. While Shepard's alerts researchers to possible problems with its treatment symbols, only you can decide the impact of an authority on the case you want to use in your analysis. Clicking on the pinpoint link for a citing source will take you to the point in that source's text where your case is cited, making it easy to determine whether the source is relevant to your research.

B. KeyCite on Westlaw

The scope of sources that can be "KeyCited" online is not identical to those that are covered under Shepard's. KeyCite is available for all cases and statutes on Westlaw. Its coverage is less complete for regulations, administrative decisions, and secondary sources. The "Scope" link provides current information about KeyCite coverage; it is located toward the bottom of the main KeyCite webpage. More state material is likely to be added over time, and checking the "Scope" link can keep you apprised of additional sources covered in KeyCite.

1. Access the Citator

KeyCite can be accessed in three different ways: through a KeyCite link at the top of a search screen, by typing a citation into the KeyCite box in the left frame, and from any source that displays a KeyCite symbol. The KeyCite link provides essential information, including an overview of analysis symbols used, a list of publications that can be updated using KeyCite, and tips on a number of KeyCite topics.

The KeyCite link connects to a page that is divided into left and right frames. The right frame explains the symbols used to show the relationship between the citing references and the authority being updated. In the left frame is a box for typing in the citation. If you do not know the citation format or whether a particular publication is included in KeyCite, click on the "Publications List" link in the left frame.

2. Select the Type of Citing List

After you enter the citation and click "Go," a list of "Full History" sources will appear in the right frame. This short list is similar to the "Shepard's for Validation" list. The first sources listed show the litigation process involving your case, i.e., the "Direct History" of the case.[9] This list of sources will show, for example, whether the case was affirmed on appeal or whether it reversed and remanded a lower court decision. Next in Full History, KeyCite lists "Negative Citing References." These are sources that KeyCite has identified as providing important negative treatment of your case. If you have limited time to update the case, you should at least skim the sources appearing under Full History. To pull up a separate window showing the actual text of a citing source, click on the number immediately preceding that source's entry in the history list. Similarly, to pull up the KeyCite page of a citing source, click on the treatment symbol (e.g., a yellow flag) preceding that source's entry in the list.

To obtain a more comprehensive list of citing sources, look in the left frame of the KeyCite screen and click on "Citing References," which is analogous to the "Shepard's for Research" list. The Citing References for the *Mendenhall* case are shown in Figure 6-7. (Notice the arrow next to "Citing References" in the left frame.)

The Citing References page first lists those citing sources that have treated your case negatively. The non-negative citing sources come next, organized according to Depth of Treatment stars. Those sources that discuss your case extensively—usually over more than one page—have been assigned four stars. As the length of the discussion of your case decreases, the number of stars is reduced. One star means that the case is merely mentioned, perhaps in a string cite. A source that quotes your case will be noted with quotation marks.

---

9. "Direct History (Graphical View)" provides that information in flowchart format.

Figure 6-7. Citing References on KeyCite

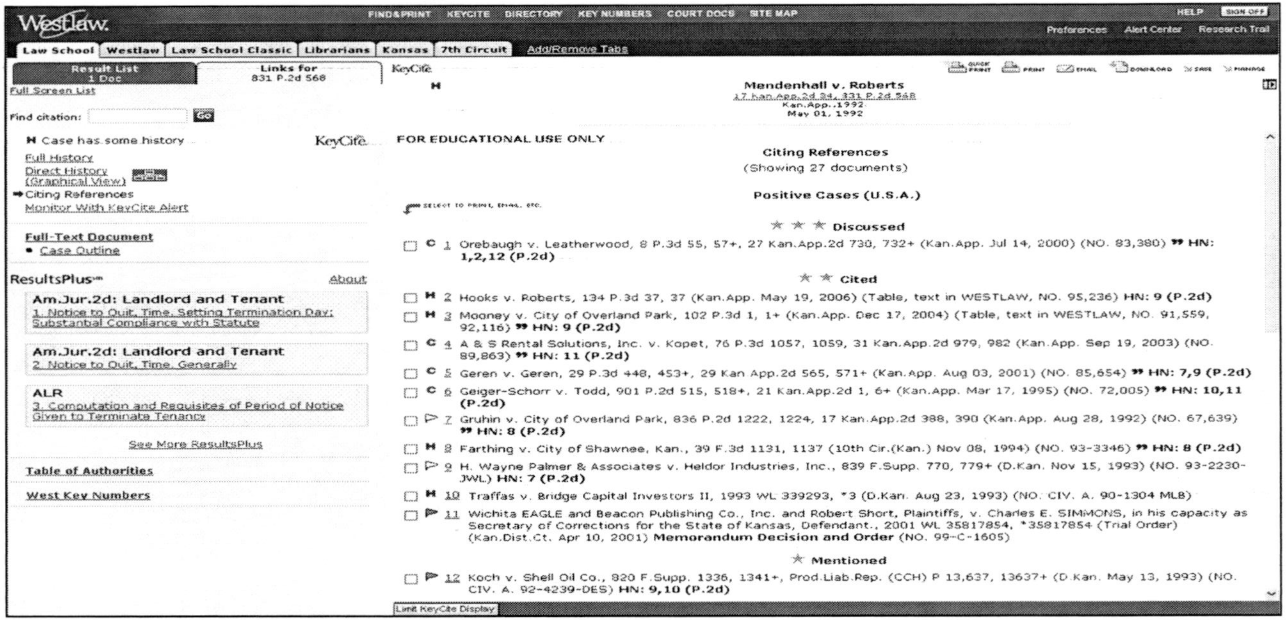

Source: Westlaw. Reprinted with permission of Thomson Reuters/West.

3. Analyze the Citator Symbols and Limit the Search Results

Similar to Shepard's, KeyCite has assigned a symbol to each authority that can be updated. The symbol is given both in the left frame and at the top-left of the right frame. This symbol is intended as a quick reference to help you determine whether the case is still good law. A summary of these symbols is provided in Table 6-4, earlier in this chapter.

Additional symbols precede each citing source. These symbols show the KeyCite assessment of the strength of each citing source, as opposed to that of the cited case. If a citing source has a negative symbol, its impact on your case may be minimal; since other sources disagree with that source, its overall authoritative value is decreased.

If your case has been cited by many sources, you may want to limit the KeyCite search results to those sources with particular relevance to your research project—e.g., sources that are from the same jurisdiction, are more recent, or address an important headnote.[10] To limit a KeyCite search in this manner, click on the "Limit KeyCite Display" button in the bottom-left of the right KeyCite frame. This will bring up a "KeyCite Limits" page. The categories of available restrictions are listed in the left frame of this page. These categories are headnotes, locate (keyword search), jurisdiction, date, document type, and depth of treatment. Clicking on a category will display that category's available restrictions in the right frame of the page. Specify all desired restrictions and then click the "Apply" button in the left frame. KeyCite will then display the filtered search results.

4. Read and Analyze the Citing Sources

Once again, the most important part of updating is reading the history cases and citing references. Reading these authorities is easy online. Clicking on an authority in the KeyCite list will take you to the point in the corresponding document where your case is cited.

---

10. As might be expected, headnotes on KeyCite correspond with the West topic and key number system.

You can quickly skim that portion of the document and decide whether the authority is relevant to your research.

III. Updating Details

A. How important are symbols?

The symbols provided by citators should be viewed as preliminary guideposts, not authoritative declarations. The law is often too complex to be captured in a simple system of symbols. A red symbol may have no impact on the point of law you are interested in, but the red often warns novice researchers away. Similarly, the absence of that symbol may provide more comfort than is warranted. Be sure to read the citing references and decide for yourself whether your case is still good law. If the case has not been explicitly overruled, consider the possibility that it has been implicitly overruled. Sound legal analysis need not be bound by the opinion of citator editors.

B. Do the symbols next to citing sources matter?

A symbol next to a citing source (before the source on KeyCite and after the source on Shepard's), refers to that source, not to the case you are updating. Thus, if you are updating the *Mendenhall* case and see that one of the cases that cites it is marked by a red symbol, that symbol is not referring to the *Mendenhall* case, but to the case citing it. Don't conclude that a case is bad law merely because one of the cases that cites it has negative treatment.

C. Which headnotes are referenced?

Sorting documents online by headnote reference requires close attention to the various sources that may publish a case. A single case may have three sets of headnotes: one set in the official reporter, a second in a West reporter (and on Westlaw), and a third set on LexisNexis.[11] Each source may have a different number of headnotes, and the substance of each headnote may be different. For example, the first headnote on LexisNexis may address a procedural point of the case while the first headnote on Westlaw may address a substantive point. Always be aware of which reporter corresponds to the headnote references in a given citator.

Similarly, even if you are working within a single family of resources (e.g., you are using Shepard's to update a case you read on LexisNexis), you must remember that headnote numbers differ among cases within that family of resources. It helps to recall that you know only the headnotes of the case that you have read, i.e., the case that you are updating—you do not know the headnotes of the citing sources. Continuing the example with the *Mendenhall* case, assume you know that headnote three of *Mendenhall* on LexisNexis is the only headnote relevant to your research project, so you restrict the Shepard's results by headnote three. Each citing source will have a headnote that summarizes the same point of law summarized in headnote three of *Mendenhall*; however, that corresponding headnote is unlikely to be the third one in the citing source. That is, while headnotes in the cited source and the citing sources address the same point of law, they will rarely match up sequentially.

D. How many cases to read?

After obtaining and analyzing the lists of citing sources, you must read every potentially relevant source in the cite list. If time allows, read *every* citing source to determine its impact on the case you are updating. Reading the citing sources in chronological order will give you a sense of how the law has developed as it was applied in various situations. If you are pressed for time, prioritize the citing sources you will read according to the following criteria:

• Focus on any negative treatment. Look for any case that reverses, overrules, criticizes, or distinguishes your case.

---

11. Unlike some state reporters, official Kansas reporters do not offer a comprehensive headnote system. They do, however, sometimes include headnotes within the official "Syllabus by the Court."

- Read cases from your jurisdiction before reading cases decided elsewhere, which are only persuasive authority.
- Read cases from the highest appellate court, then the intermediate appellate courts, and finally the trial courts (if trial court cases are published) in the jurisdiction.
- Start with more recent cases rather than older cases.
- Choose cases cited for the headnotes that are on point for your research.

E. What is the Table of Authorities?

Both Shepard's and KeyCite provide a link from their updating pages to a case's "Table of Authorities." This function lists the cases cited by the case being updated; in other words, it looks back, while updating looks forward.

The Table of Authorities is valuable first because it provides a list of cases that you may need to read. If the case you are updating relied on these cases, they may be relevant to your research in their own right. Second, the Table of Authorities indicates whether the cases in that list are still respected. If they are not, the case you are updating may be on shaky ground because authority it relied on is no longer valid. Note that the original citator analysis might not reflect this troubling possibility. However, resist the temptation to burn valuable research time on this analysis early in the research process. The Table of Authorities should typically be consulted toward the end of the research process when the legal issues and relevant authorities have been clearly defined.

IV. When to Update

Updating is a valuable research tool at several points in the research process. Always check the colored symbol of a case you are reading online so that you will know immediately whether the case has been treated negatively. If so, you may want to explore that treatment before beginning to place much reliance on the case's analysis.

Later, when you have determined that a case is relevant to your research, carefully review its list of citing sources to find other cases and secondary sources that discuss the same points of law as the first case. Reading the citing sources produced by an updating search may lead to cases in which the court's reasoning is explained more fully or to cases with facts more similar to yours.

As you discover more cases that are on point for your issue, look for trends in frequency and treatment of case citations. In general, cases that have been cited frequently and followed extensively should form the basis of your analysis. A case that has been ignored by later cases may be excluded from your analysis unless the facts are very similar to yours or the reasoning is especially relevant. A line of cases that criticize or distinguish your case will have to be countered in your analysis.

You should continue updating cases and other authorities until the moment your final document is submitted. Shepard's and KeyCite are continually publishing updated information; the case you updated two weeks ago could have been overruled yesterday.

V. Ethics

Courts expect lawyers to Shepardize to ensure that their arguments are supported and present the current state of the law to the courts. "[F]ailure to 'Shepardize' a key case [is] not excusable."[12]

Failing to cite current law or disclose adverse authority may result in sanctions, malpractice suits, public embarrassment, and damage to your reputation. Kansas Rule of Professional Conduct (KRPC) 3.3(a)(2) states that a lawyer shall not knowingly "fail to disclose to the tribunal legal authority in the controlling jurisdiction known to the lawyer to be directly adverse to the position of the client and not disclosed by opposing counsel...." The comments for this rule explain that a "lawyer is not required to make a disinterested exposition of the law, but must recognize the existence of pertinent legal authorities."

---

12. *McCarthy v. Oregon Freeze Dry, Inc.*, 158 Or. App. 654, 656 (1999).

In one instance, a judge ordered a major law firm to copy for each of its partners and associates an opinion chastising the firm for failing to cite a case adverse to the client's argument.[13] In another case, an attorney was suspended from practice for failure to file the client's claim within the limitations period. In reviewing the facts of the case, the court noted that the attorney "had not Shepardized the cases he relied on regarding the statute of limitations."[14]

---

13. *Golden Eagle Distribg. Corp. v. Burroughs Corp.*, 103 F.R.D. 124, 129 (N.D. Cal. 1984) ("For counsel to have been unaware of those cases means that they did not Shepardize their principal authority....").

14. *In re Tway*, 919 P.2d 323, 325 (Idaho 1996).

Chapter 7

Statutes

Statutes affect a multitude of legal issues.[1] Often a statute defines a client's rights or responsibilities. A statute may set penalties for failure to comply with the statutory mandate.

Table 7-1 outlines the general process of researching Kansas statutes in print and online.

I. Kansas Statutory Research

Laws enacted since the beginning of statehood that are still valid are compiled and organized by subject matter (codified) into *Kansas Statutes Annotated* (KSA). Before any copies of a volume of the KSA are printed and bound, they must be examined and compared by the secretary of state and by the attorney general. If they contain all the laws required, they are certified. After this authentication, they are held to be the official statutes of Kansas.[2]

Distinct subject areas in *Kansas Statutes Annotated* are designated as chapters. Although it appears there are 84 chapters in KSA, in fact, there are 89, since five additional chapters have been inserted. Chapters are composed of articles, which in turn are composed of sections.

---

1. This chapter explains how to research Kansas state statutes. County and city codes are increasingly available online. Blue Skyways, a service of the Kansas State Library, connects to Kansas county and city information at http://skyways.lib.ks.us/index.html. Some county and city codes are available on LexisNexis and Westlaw.

2. K.S.A. 77-137.

Table 7-1. Kansas Statutory Research

1. Generate a comprehensive list of research terms.
2. Look in the *General Index to the Kansas Statutes Annotated* under the research terms to find relevant statutes. Alternatively, search online by reviewing the table of contents, skimming an online index, or conducting a full-text search.
3. Read the statutory text, either in print or online. Using *Kansas Statutes Annotated* in print, look in the appropriate KSA bound volume for the chapter and section; find current changes by turning to the supplementary pamphlets.
4. Read annotations to find citations to cases and other authorities that interpret, apply, or analyze the statute. In KSA and most online sources, the annotations follow the language of the statute.
5. Read and analyze the relevant cases.
6. Look in the Statutes Appealed or Amended Table in the back of the most recent volume of the *Session Laws of Kansas*, which comes out in July, to see if the KSA section has been repealed or amended by the acts in the current volume of the session laws.

A. The Research Process Using KSA in Print

A chapter-article-section numbering system is used for Kansas statutes.[3] To take a current example, the "75" in KSA 75-101 stands for Chapter 75. Moving left to right, the first "1" stands for Article 1 and the next "01" stands for Section 1. If the sections in an article exceed 99, the section numbers are preceded by a comma and will read as a unit (75-1, 101, read as Chapter 75, Article 1, Section 101). Under this alphabetical chapter-classification system used since 1923,

---

3. This system was first used in Kansas in the *Revised Statutes of 1923* and has continued through the later versions of *General Statutes of Kansas* and *Kansas Statutes Annotated*.

it is not possible in many cases to find all of the statutes pertaining to the same subject matter in the same chapter or article. Therefore, numerous "Cross References to Related Sections" have been inserted by the Revisor of Statutes to facilitate finding the location of statutes that are closely related but that appear elsewhere in KSA.

Most chapters are divided into articles. All articles in a chapter are listed in order at the beginning of the chapter. If the researcher is acquainted with the subject being researched and is sure that it is covered in a particular chapter, scanning the list of articles is a quick way to locate the information wanted. In most situations, however, the subject index is a more reliable means of reaching an appropriate section.

1. Develop a List of Research Terms

To find all the statutes that may relate to your project, develop an expansive list of research terms. Use the journalistic approach or the TARPP method from Chapter 1, or design a brainstorming technique that works for you.

2. Search the Index

Take these research terms to the index volume that is shelved at the end of the KSA volumes. Search for every one of your research terms. As you find the terms in the index volume, write down any statutory references given.

Do not stop reviewing the index after finding just one statute reference; several statutes may address your issue. Note that *et seq.* refers to the statute listed and the sections that follow it. Sometimes a research term will be included in the index but will be followed by a cross-reference to another index term. Referring to that term may lead you to relevant statutes.

The KSA index contains a boldface heading entitled WORDS AND PHRASES. This heading includes index entries of all words or phrases that are defined in sections of KSA. Researchers looking for definitions relating to a specific area of the law should look under the subheading "Definitions" under the specific boldface heading. For example, to find definitions used in income tax law, look under the boldface heading INCOME TAX, subheading "Definitions." Section 201 (Rules of Construction) under Article 2 (Statutory Construction) of Chapter 77 (Statutes) also details how certain words, phrases, and terms found throughout the statutes are to be construed.

The KSA index also contains a boldface heading entitled POPU-LAR NAME LAWS. This heading is particularly helpful for locating the statutory citation of named acts or acts commonly referred to by another name. For example, to find the citation to the Automobile Injury Reparations Act, commonly known as the No-fault Insurance Law, look under entries "Automobile Injury Reparations Act, 40-3101 *et seq.*" and "No-fault insurance, Automobile Injury Reparations Act, 40-3101 *et seq.*"

3. Find and Read the Statutory Language

For each statutory citation you found in the index, select the volume of KSA that contains the chapter of your statute, and then find the statute itself.

This next step is the most important: *Read the statute very carefully.* Too many researchers fail to take the time necessary to read the language of the statute and consider all its implications before deciding whether it is relevant to a research problem. And because few statutes are so clear that they can be understood on one reading, careful research may require you to read a statute several times to understand its meaning and relevance.

To understand a single statute you may have to read other related statutes. One statue may contain general provisions while another contains definitions. Yet another statute may contain exceptions to the general rule.

In the example in Figure 7-2, the statute prohibits disposal of solid wastes, but then refers to other statutes. KSA 65-3424 notes the exception for waste tires and defines important terms. Additionally, KSA 65-3407c lists exemptions from the permit requirement for waste facilities.

There is no guarantee that any researcher will understand all statutes, especially if conflict is involved. You will, nonetheless, enhance the chances for understanding significantly by breaking the

Figure 7-2. Example Kansas Statute

65-3409 Unlawful acts; penalties.

(a) It shall be unlawful for any person to:

(1) Dispose of any solid waste by open dumping, but this provision shall not prohibit: (A) The use of solid wastes, except for waste tires, as defined by KSA 65-3424, and amendments thereto, in normal farming operations or in the processing or manufacturing of other products in a manner that will not create a public nuisance or adversely affect the public health; or (B) an individual from dumping or depositing solid wastes resulting from such individual's own residential or agricultural activities onto the surface of land owned or leased by such individual when such wastes do not create a public nuisance or adversely affect the public health or the environment.

(2) Except as **otherwise provided** by KSA 65-3407c, and amendments thereto, construct, alter or operate a solid waste processing or disposal facility or act as a waste tire transporter or mobile waste tire processor, as **defined** by KSA 65-3424, and amendments thereto, without a permit or be in violation of the rules and regulations, standards or orders of the secretary.

Source: *Kansas Statutes Annotated*, volume 5, page 420 (2002) (emphasis added). Used with permission of the Revisor of Statutes of the State of Kansas.

statute into elements. Using bullet points or an outline format is helpful for identifying key ideas. Some statutory sentence structure can be very complex. Connecting words and punctuation can provide guidance for the relationships between the different requirements of a statute. In addition, most statutes are filled with legal terminology. The thoughtful researcher will have a law dictionary always within reach.

4. Find Cases that Interpret or Apply the Statute

Understanding statutes is aided by researching cases since many statutes have already been interpreted by the courts. Legislatures write statutes generally to apply to a wide array of circumstances. To be able to predict how a court may apply a statute to a client's specific facts, you must know how the courts have interpreted the statute and applied it in the past.

After most statutory sections in KSA, there are annotations to Kansas Supreme Court and Kansas Court of Appeals decisions that have interpreted, construed, or merely applied the statutory section. Each annotation consists of a short summary of a point of law, the case name, and the citation of the case. You must record the citation information accurately to be able to find the cases in the reporters or online. KSA does not include annotations to federal court decisions that have interpreted Kansas statutes.

After most statutes, appearing before the case annotations, you will find *Research and Practice Aids*. These include references to West's topic-key number digest system; legal encyclopedias, *American Jurisprudence 2d* and *Corpus Juris Secundum*; and current forms and practice books applicable to Kansas, most of which are published by Thomson/West.

Law Reviews and Bar Journal Reference appears after *Research and Practice Aids* and *Attorney General's Opinions* but before the case annotations. This section contains citations to the *Journal of the Kansas Bar Association*, *University of Kansas Law Review*, *Washburn Law Journal*, *Journal of the Kansas Trial Lawyer Association*, and *Kansas Journal of Law and Public Policy*.

5. Other Helpful Features of KSA

Previous legislation generally appears in the form of a "Source or Prior Law" or a "Revisor's Note." Following the "Source or Prior Law" or "Revisor's Notes" are the Research and Practice Aids discussed above.

A legislative history follows each statutory section and includes the effective date of the legislation and the effective date of amendments, if any. For example, the history following KSA 21-3601 reads: "History: L. 1969, ch. 180, §21-3601; L. 1992, ch. 239, §87; L. 1993, ch. 291, §54, July 1." This history means that the section was originally enacted in 1969, was assigned section number 21-3601 in *Kansas Statutes Annotated*, and has been amended twice, once in 1992 and once in 1993. The 1993 amendment became effective July 1, 1993.

Somewhat curiously, references are still made in KSA to *Hatcher's Digest*, which was last supplemented in 1975. A researcher can go from a *Hatcher's Digest* topic to the equivalent *Kansas Digest* topic by noting where a case digested in *Hatcher's* is digested in the *Kansas Digest*.

B. Kansas Statutes Online

1. State Website

The state legislature maintains a very helpful website at www.kslegislature.org. The site index provides a statutes tab on the left-hand side that links to an online version of the unannotated Kansas statutes. The online version of the Kansas statutes is not official, even though the text is provided with the permission of the Revisor of Statutes for the State of Kansas and is maintained by the state. In any discrepancy, rely on the print version of *Kansas Statutes Annotated*.

If you know which one of the 89 chapters is relevant to the research, simply click on the correct chapter. All the articles in that chapter will then be listed. By clicking on a particular article, you will see the various statute numbers under that article. A particular statute will come up by clicking on the statute number.

The site has a rudimentary search engine. You can type in the statute number or keyword or phrase. If searching by keyword or phrase, the results will be sorted by relevance.

2. Kansas Statutes on Westlaw

Kansas statutes are available on Westlaw in several databases. When you know the statute's number, go to the "Find by citation" box in the left frame of your screen and type in "KS-ST" and the number (the official abbreviation for Westlaw is KS-ST, which is provided in the "Publications List" link). If you are viewing Westlaw on split screen, the text of the statute will appear in the right frame. Farther down that frame is the "History." Clicking on "Table of Contents" in the left frame will show where the statute is located within the Kansas statutes, providing context.

To begin statutory research without citations for relevant statutes, you can review the KS-ST table of contents, search Westlaw's index for Kansas statutes, or conduct a full-text search. To begin with the

KS-ST table of contents, click the "Table of Contents" link next to Kansas statutes under the Kansas tab. Clicking on a box with an "+" will expand the table of contents from chapters to articles and ultimately individual statutes. By selecting a particular chapter or article and clicking on "Search" at the bottom of the screen, you can search that particular portion of KS-ST for your terms. Note that this search is different from searching the actual table of contents, which is possible on LexisNexis.

To search Westlaw's index, click on "Statutes Index" under the Kansas tab. You will have a choice of typing a term into a search box or scrolling through a portion of the alphabetical index. Links lead to statutory citations or to other terms cross-referenced in the index. Alternatively, the index also provides a link to statutes by popular names.

To conduct a full-text search, use the Kansas tab or go to the Westlaw "Directory" and follow the link to Kansas statutory databases. Click the "i" icon to see what is included in each database and how current it is. In the search box, type either a terms and connectors search or a natural language search. Each document the search retrieves may have both a statute and its annotations, though your research terms may appear in just the annotations, not the statute.

3. Kansas Statutes on LexisNexis

LexisNexis provides Kansas statutes in a database called "LexisNexis Kansas Annotated Statutes." To begin researching with a statute's number, click on the "Get a Document" tab and type "Kan. Stat. Ann." followed by the statute number. Clicking on "TOC" at the top left of your screen will lead to a screen that shows your statute and the surrounding statutes, including their chapters and articles.

Without a statute's number, you can search either the Kan. Stat. Ann. Table of Contents or the full text of Kansas statutes. First, go to a list of the Kansas databases. If you have created a Kansas tab, simply click on it. An alternative approach is to click on "Search" at the top left of the screen, then "States Legal-U.S.," and then "Kansas." (You may need to click on "View more sources" to see the Kansas databases.) Next, select a Kansas database, such as "KS-LexisNexis Kansas Annotated Statutes." Searching a larger database, for example, "KS-Kansas Statutes Annotated, Constitution, Court Rules & ALS, Combined," may not provide the focused documents that you need. Again, to learn what a database contains and how current it is, click on the "i" icon for information.

To access the table of contents, select a database, and then click on the "Table of Contents (TOC) only" option. Enter your research terms in the text field, and click the "Search" button.

To search the full text of the statutes using research terms or a phrase, select the "Full-Text of Source Documents" option instead. Note that, in a full-text search, your results may include documents with your search terms in the text of a statute, or in an annotation referring to a case or law review article. Read carefully and do not assume that each hit uses your research terms in a statute's text.

II. Applying and Interpreting Kansas Statutes

The meaning of a particular statute in Kansas depends upon the intent of the legislature.

Interpretation of a statute is a question of law. Under the fundamental rule of statutory construction, the intent of the legislature governs when that intent can be ascertained from the statute. When a statute is plain and unambiguous, an appellate court must give effect to the intention of the legislature, rather than determine what the law should or should not be. "The general rule is that a criminal statute must be strictly construed in favor of the accused, which means that words are given their ordinary meaning. Any reasonable doubt about the meaning is decided in favor of anyone subjected to the criminal statute." The rule of strict construction, however, is subordinate to the rule that judicial interpretation must be reasonable and sensible to effect legislative design and intent.[4]

---

4. *State v. Cox*, 258 Kan. 557, 577–78 (1995) (citations omitted).

III. Federal Statutes

The official text of federal statutes is published in the *United States Code* (USC). Federal statutes are codified in USC under fifty titles. Within each title, individual statutes are assigned section numbers. To cite a federal statute, include both the title and the section number. The federal statute granting appellate jurisdiction to federal appellate courts is 28 USC § 1291 (2006). Title 28 is devoted to courts and judicial matters, and 1291 is the section number assigned to this statute. The date of publication of that volume of USC was 2006.

USC is updated infrequently and does not include annotations, so it is of limited value in research. The more commonly used print sources are *United States Code Annotated* (USCA) and *United States Code Service* (USCS). If the current text of the statute is not yet available in USC, citing USCA or USCS is preferred over citing an online source. Even if you use LexisNexis, Westlaw, or another online source to find a federal statute, cite it to one of the print codifications listed above.

Both USCA and USCS contain the text of federal statutes and references to related research sources. Both USCA and USCS include annotations that refer to cases interpreting or applying each federal statute. Some researchers feel that USCA provides more case annotations than USCS, while USCS provides more helpful tables and better information on court rules. Often the two are of equal value, so use whichever one is available.

USCA and USCS are updated through pocket parts and paperback supplements. When only portions of a statute have changed, the pocket part may refer to the unchanged language in the hardbound volume. Other pocket parts are cumulative, so a modified statute will be reprinted in full. Some researchers prefer to begin with the pocket part information, focusing on the most recent statutory language and annotations, and then refer back to the bound volume.

Both annotated code publications contain information other than statutes and research annotations. For example, they provide references to federal regulations and executive orders. Both USCS and USCA include tables listing statutes by their popular names. And as explained in the next part, both contain federal court rules.

IV. Court Rules

Court rules have the force of law governing practice and procedure in the courts. They cover procedures in the trial court system (rules of civil and criminal procedure), govern procedures before a specific court (e.g., Kansas Supreme Court Rules), and govern certain aspects of the rules of evidence. There are also housekeeping rules with specific practices required by a court.

A. Kansas Court Rules

Rules of the Kansas Supreme Court are not statutory law, but they are printed as directed by KSA 77-132 in the single volume *Rules Adopted by the Supreme Court of the State of Kansas*. All of the Kansas Supreme Court Rules are no longer printed in the *Kansas Statutes Annotated*. Rather, you will find the *Rules Adopted by the Supreme Court of the State of Kansas* published annually under the authority of law by the direction of the Supreme Court of Kansas. A popular source for the rules is the *Kansas Court Rules and Procedure* by West. *Rules Adopted by the Supreme Court of the State of Kansas* can also be obtained over the Internet on the Kansas Judicial Branch website at www.kscourts.org. Consult the latest bound volumes of the *Rules* adopted by the Supreme Court of Kansas and advance sheets to get the latest official text of a rule.

The appellate court rules (or rules relating to Supreme Court, Court of Appeals, and appellate practice) are also published in Appendix A of S. Gard and R. Casad, *Kansas Code of Civil Procedure 4th Annotated* (Thomson/West, 2003 & Supp.). These rules are also available on the Kansas Judicial Branch website at www.kscourts.org.

The rules of the Supreme Court relating to district courts in Kansas are also in Appendix B of Gard and Casad's book. These rules are also available on the Kansas Judicial Branch website at www.kscourts.org. The district court link on the website features individual district court pages. Some of these pages offer their own district local court rules.

The Kansas Code of Civil Procedure is statutory law and became effective in 1964. Justice of the peace courts, county courts, and other courts of limited jurisdiction were abolished. An integrated district court system came into existence so that limited actions fall within the jurisdiction of the district court and become the special responsibility of magistrate associate district judges. The Code of Civil Procedure is in Chapter 60 of volume 4A of KSA. The rules of civil procedure are in Article 60-2. These rules govern civil procedure for the district courts of Kansas other than for actions commenced pursuant to Chapter 61 of KSA (civil procedure for limited actions). The civil procedure rules run from 60-201 through 60-271. KSA 60-269 contains forms that are intended for illustration but are expressly declared by KSA 60-268 to be sufficient for actual use. Gard and Casad in Appendix C of their book also have forms for civil procedure that duplicate those in KSA. There is also a Code of Civil Procedure for Limited Actions instead of a code for courts of limited jurisdiction. The rules of civil procedure for limited actions are in Article 17 of Chapter 61 of KSA. There is an appendix of forms at KSA 61-2605 with forms for summons, garnishment, etc. There are also Chapter 61 forms on the Kansas Judicial council website at www.kscourts.org/council.

Kansas rules of criminal procedure are not specified as such. However, the Kansas Code of Criminal Procedure is found at KSA 22-2101 et seq. At the time of the recommendation of the criminal code by the Advisory Committee in 1969, it was thought that the term "Rules of Criminal Procedure" might be used as the title to Chapter 22 of KSA, thus providing the ready reference to "Code" for Chapter 21 (which deals with crimes and punishments) and "Rules" for Chapter 22 (which deals with criminal procedure). This usage was not adopted, however.

The Kansas Rules of Evidence are codified at KSA 60-401 et seq. The Kansas Rules of Evidence follow the 1953 Uniform Rules of Evidence. Kansas is the only state to have adopted the 1953 Uniform Rules of Evidence. The Uniform Rules played a part in influencing the pattern of the Federal Rules of Evidence enacted and promulgated in 1975, but there are many differences. For this reason, Kansas prac-

titioners need to be aware of both the Kansas Rules based on the 1953
Uniform Rules and the dissimilar Federal Rules of Evidence.

B. Federal Court Rules

Similar court rules exist on the federal level and they are published
in similar sources. In Appendix E of their book, Gard and Casad list
the Federal Rules of Civil Procedure for the U.S. District Courts. A
very good source of court rules for the U.S. District Court for the District of Kansas is *Federal Local Court Rules* (3d ed., Thomson/West
2001). Court rules are also published in *Kansas Rules of Court: Federal* as well as in USC, USCA, and USCS; placement of the rules
varies among the statutory publications. In USC and USCA, for example, the Federal Rules of Appellate Procedure appear just after Title
28. In USCS, those rules are found at the end of all fifty titles in separate volumes devoted to rules. Federal court rules are available on
LexisNexis and Westlaw. Additionally, courts frequently post their
rules on their websites. For example, the Supreme Court's rules are
on its website at www.supremecourtus.gov. As at the state level, each
federal court may have its own "local rules" with specific practices required by that court.

Cases relevant to federal rules can be located using the annotated
codes, or by referring to *Federal Practice Digest*, *Federal Rules Service*
(rules of procedure), and *Federal Rules of Evidence Service*.

Chapter 8

Legislative History

I. The Legislative Process

This chapter begins with an overview of the legislative process in Kansas through which the statutory laws of Kansas are enacted. Next, the chapter explains how to research the *legislative history* of a statute. Legislative history research is most often relevant in litigation when an attorney needs to convince a court to interpret an ambiguous statute in a way that is favorable to the client's position. Understanding the legislative process is important because the process produces documents that may help determine the legislature's intent in passing a statute, which is a key to statutory interpretation. Legislative history can be especially important when a court is interpreting a statute for the first time.

The Kansas Legislature (also called the Assembly) consists of two houses—a House of Representatives, with 125 members, and a Senate, with forty members. The Assembly meets for regular sessions each year. The general process of enacting or amending laws in Kansas is similar to that of other states and the United States Congress. Figure 8-1 shows the basic steps a Kansas bill goes through to become law.

II. Kansas Legislative History

Most statutory text is clear in both language and intent. However, due to the vagaries of language, ambiguity will sometimes make the

Figure 8-1. How a Bill Becomes Law

A bill may be introduced in either the House of Representatives or the Senate. The main steps in the process of a bill becoming a law are shown below.

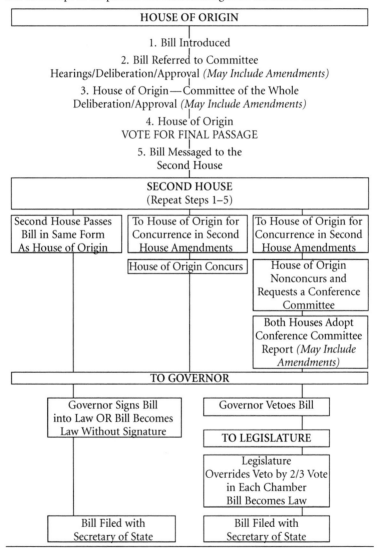

Source: www.kslegislature.org. Used with permission of the Kansas Legislative Research Department.

meaning of a statute unclear. Legislative history may give critical support for a particular construction of a statute that favors an attorney's client. In Kansas, the burden is on the attorney to ask the court to interpret an ambiguous statute, in contrast to some federal courts, where courts will sometimes take the initiative. If the Kansas court agrees with the attorney regarding possible ambiguities, the Kansas court will then use legislative history to determine the intent of a statute.

In *In re Appeal of University of Kansas School of Medicine-Wichita Medical Practice Association*,[1] the Kansas Supreme Court noted:

> [w]hen a statute is plain and unambiguous, a court must give effect to the intention of the legislature as expressed.... However, where the face of the statute leaves its construction uncertain, the court may properly look into the historical background of the enactment, the circumstances attending its passage, the purpose to be accomplished, and the effect the statute may have under various constructions suggested.[2]

III. Finding Legislative History in Kansas

A. Systematic Approach for Kansas Sources

As in many other states, finding legislative history in Kansas can be a frustrating endeavor. The sources are limited and not always easily accessible. This section presents a systematic approach[3] that should help reduce frustration. Specific sources (minutes, interim studies, and journals) will be addressed below in step five.

---

1. 266 Kan. 737 (1999).
2. *Id.* at 749–50 (citations omitted).
3. Based on Richard E. Levy & Robert Mead, *Using Legislative History as a Tool of Statutory Construction in Kansas*, 71 J. Kan. B. Assn. 35, 41–43 (May 2002).

1. Retrieve the Statute and its Predecessors

Since legislative history is focused on a particular statute, it only makes sense that research starts with the statute. The current annotated statutes printed in *Kansas Statutes Annotated* provide a condensed legislative history for each statute. The history includes the *Session Laws of Kansas* citation, the enactment date, and (since statutes are evolutionary in nature) any citations to earlier statutory versions. See the history section[4] following KSA 21-3404 in Figure 8-2.

2. Research Prior Judicial Interpretations of the Statute

Kansas courts adhere to *stare decisis* regarding prior judicial construction of a statute.[5] It is very unlikely that a court will re-interpret an earlier statute interpretation.[6] Consequently, the next step should be to check the annotations of the target statute for prior judicial interpretations (even if they are not directly on point). This step will provide a shortcut to possible essential documents or information.

3. Research the Session Laws that Amended the Target Statute

Next, research any pertinent *Session Laws of Kansas* volumes to identify the particular enactment in which the language to be interpreted first appeared.[7] In addition, make note of any other textual changes that are cited.[8]

Each chapter of the *Session Laws of Kansas* gives bill numbers essential for finding committee minutes (discussed below). The *Session*

---

4. L. 1969, ch. 180 21-3404. "L. 1969" refers to the 1969 volume edition of the *Session Laws of Kansas*. "Ch. 180" refers to the 180th chapter in the 1969 *Session Laws of Kansas*. "§ 21-3404" refers to the statute in *Kansas Statutes Annotated* that the session law was assigned.

5. *In re Adoption of B.M.W.*, 268 Kan. 871 (2000); *In re Adoption of K.J.B.*, 265 Kan. 90 (1998).

6. Levy & Mead, *supra* n. 3, at 41.

7. *Id.*

8. *Id.*

Figure 8-2. History of a Kansas Statute

21-3404. Involuntary manslaughter. Involuntary manslaughter is the unintentional killing of a human being committed:

(a) Recklessly;

(b) in the commission of, or attempt to commit, or flight from any felony, other than an inherently dangerous felony as defined in K.S.A. 21-3436 and amendments thereto, that is enacted for the protection of human life or safety or a misdemeanor that is enacted for the protection of human life or safety, including acts described in K.S.A. 8-1566 and subsection (a) of 8-1568, and amendments thereto, but excluding the acts described in K.S.A. 8-1567 and amendments thereto; or

(c) during the commission of a lawful act in an unlawful manner.

Involuntary manslaughter is a severity level 5, person felony.

History: L. 1969, ch. 180, § 21-3404; L. 1979, ch. 90, § 3; L. 1982, ch. 132, § 2; L. 1992, ch. 298, § 6; L. 1993, ch. 291, § 21; L. 1996, ch. 158, § 2; L. 2005, ch. 59, § 1; July 1.

Source or prior law:
21-407, 21-410, 21-411, 21-412, 21-413, 21-414, 21-415, 21-418, 21-419, 21-420.

Law Review and Bar Journal References:
"Survey of Kansas Law: Criminal Procedure," Keith G. Meyer, 27 K.L.R. 391, 439 (1979).

"Criminal Law: The Kansas Approach to the Battered Woman's Use of Self-Defense [State v. Hundley, 236 Kan. 461, 693 P.2d 475 (1985)]," Shelley A. Ryan, 25 W.L.J. 174, 176, 178 (1985).

"Corporate Criminal Liability for Injuries and Death," Patrick Hamilton, 40 K.L.R. 1091, 1105, 1106 (1992).

"Solidifying the Use of Juvenile Proceedings as Sentence Enhancement and Clarifying Second-Degree Murder," Kay Redeker, 37 W.L.J. 483 (1998).

Source: *Kansas Statutes Annotated.* Used with permission of the Revisor of Statutes of the State of Kansas.

Laws of Kansas are also marked with strike-through and italicized font, which can be illustrative of legislative intent. "Material added to an existing section of a statute is printed in italic type. Material deleted from an existing section of the statute is printed in canceled type."[9]

4. Identify and Analyze Bills

The evolution of the bill should be examined. Comparison of different bill versions may support an argument regarding legislative intent based on the addition or deletion of language as the bill went through the legislative process. A finalized bill with strike-through font indicates the bill had included canceled-out language prior to amendment. Language in bold font indicates language added through amendment. As with *Session Laws of Kansas*, discussed above, any change in language can indicate legislative intent. Supplemental Notes, prepared by the Legislative Research Department,[10] are attached to the bills and are discussed below.

5. Check Interim Studies, Committee Minutes, and Journals

The Kansas Legislature, unlike Congress, does not publish committee reports for standing committees. However, during the interim period between sessions, the Legislative Coordinating Council[11] selects study topics for the special committees and the Legislative Research Department to study.

Interim studies typically analyze policy objectives and alternate means of obtaining them, including alternative formulations of

---

9. This language appears in explanatory notes at the beginning of each volume of *Session Laws of Kansas*.

10. The Legislative Research Department is a nonpartisan agency that provides support services for the Kansas Legislature.

11. The Legislative Coordinating Council is a creature of a statute, K.S.A. 46-1210. Its authority and power to act are clearly delineated by the Kansas Legislature.

statutes.[12] Kansas courts take note of interim studies when looking for legislative intent. There is a cumulative subject index for interim studies, but it is not widely available.[13] Beginning with 1974, the first place to look for a report or an interim study concerning a particular bill is the Supplemental Note (or information) on the bill, usually bound with the bill itself. The Supplemental Notes do not provide legislative history, but they can provide useful information about each bill.

Another source of legislative intent in Kansas can be found in the committee minutes of legislative committees that heard the bill. Minutes include what went on in the committee hearings: statements by committee members, testimony by witnesses and questions asked of them, and written testimony. The minutes are a summary of all this, although the written testimony is usually in complete form and simply attached to the minutes. Individual remarks are not recorded verbatim.[14]

The quality of the minutes varies from committee to committee, although a standard form has been used since 1970.[15] The minutes are on microfiche located on the fifth floor in the Legislative Administration Service office in the State Capitol. For attorneys outside the Topeka area, the Legislative Administration Service will ship copies of minutes for a fee.[16] Unofficial versions retrospective to 2000 are available on the Internet. The online coverage is spotty, depending on the committee.

12. Levy & Mead, *supra* n. 3, at 42.

13. University of Kansas Wheat Law School Library, University of Washburn Law Library, Kansas Supreme Court Law Library, and the Kansas State Library (retrospective to 1934) contain cumulative subject indexes.

14. The following statement is on the form used to record the minutes: "Unless specifically noted, the individual remarks recorded herein have not been transcribed verbatim. Individual remarks as reported herein have not been submitted to the individuals appearing before the committee for editing or corrections."

15. Fritz Snyder & Joyce A. McCray Pearson, Chapter Three: Researching Legislative Intent, in *Kansas Legal Research and Reference Guide* (Joseph A. Custer ed., 2d ed., KBA Pub. 1997).

16. The Legislative Administrative Service's phone number is (785) 296-2391.

The *Kansas Senate Journal* and *Kansas House Journal* are records of day-to-day legislative operations, including committee and floor votes in addition to proposed amendments. These sources allow a researcher to trace the movement of a bill through the legislative process. An example of how the *Journals* could be useful would be to research proposed amendments to a bill. Following this research with a thorough consideration of the accepted and rejected bill amendments may offer indications of legislative intent.

While the *Journals* do not include the text of floor debates, they do include any recorded reason a legislator may have given for voting a certain way. The *Journals* also include text from the governor, which may include reasons for recommending legislation and vetoing other legislation.

B. Kansas Free Online Sources

The Kansas Legislature's website at www.kslegislature.org contains much of the material explained above, but only for recent years.

C. Kansas Legislative History on Westlaw and LexisNexis

Westlaw has a database called "Kansas Legislature Old" (KS-LEGIS-OLD), which covers acts and resolutions passed by the Kansas Legislature from 1991 to and through all sessions except those of the two most recent years. The "Kansas Legislative Service" (KS-LEGIS) database contains session laws.

LexisNexis's database "Kansas Legislative Bill History" (KSLH) contains helpful insight into the legislative history of a particular bill, ballot measure, executive order, amendment, or other legislation. The legislative history documents include: bill analysis, governors' messages, committee reports, fiscal messages, summary amendments, and other types. Coverage starts in 2005. "Kansas Advanced Legislative Services" (KSALS) contains session laws from 1988 to present.

D. Bill Tracking

Bill tracking is the opposite of legislative history. While legislative history looks back in time to learn about a statute that has already been enacted, bill tracking follows a current bill as it makes its way through the legislature.

If you know the number of a bill you need to track, you can do this also on the Kansas Legislature's website by typing in the bill number. The bill information includes the full history of a current bill. If you are a paying subscriber, you can pay $1.00 and view the status of up to five bills as they progress through the session.

Bill tracking is possible in Westlaw by researching the database "Kansas Bill Tracking-Summaries & Full Text Combined" (KS-BILLS). Smaller databases provide specific material, for example the text of bills.

Bill tracking is also available on LexisNexis. The database "Kansas Bill Tracking and Full-Text Bills" (KSBILL) provides bill tracking reports and texts of bills for the current legislative session.

IV. Federal Legislative Research

Researching federal legislative history involves roughly the same steps as researching Kansas laws, though some of the terminology is different. Federal bills are numbered sequentially in each chamber of Congress. Generally, Senate bill numbers are preceded by an "S." and House of Representatives bill numbers are preceded by "H.R." When a federal statute is enacted, it is assigned a *public law number*. This number is in the form Pub. L. No. 101-336, where the numerals before the hyphen are the number of the Congress in which the law was enacted and the numerals after the hyphen are assigned chronologically as bills are enacted. The public law number given above is for the Americans with Disabilities Act (ADA), which was passed in 1990 during the 101st Congress.

The new statute is later published as a *session law* in *United States Statutes at Large*, which is the federal counterpart of the *Session Laws*

Table 8-3. Selected Resources for Federal Legislative History in Print

Resource	Contents
United States Code Congressional and Administrative News (USCCAN)	Selected reprints and excerpts of committee reports; references to other reports and to the *Congressional Record*
Congressional Information Service (CIS)	Full text of bills, committee reports, and hearings on microfiche; print indexes and abstracts in bound volumes
Congressional Record	Debate from the floor of the House and Senate

of Kansas. Session laws are designated by volume and page in *Statutes at Large*, e.g., 104 Stat. 328. Finally, the new statute is assigned a *statute number* when it is codified with statutes on similar topics in the *United State Code.* The citation for the first section of the ADA is 42 U.S.C. § 12101.

As with Kansas legislative history, federal legislative history research begins with a statute number. If you do not know the statute number, use an annotated code to find it (as described in Chapter 7). With a statute number, you can find the session law citation and the public law number, which will lead to the legislative history of the bill as it worked its way through Congress.

A. Sources of Federal Legislative History

The goal of federal legislative history research is to find committee reports, materials from committee hearings, and transcripts of floor debates. Sources for these documents are summarized in Table 8-3. Committee reports are considered the most persuasive authority; they are often lengthy documents. These reports contain the committee's analysis of the bill, the reasons for enacting it, and the views of any members who disagree with those reasons. Congressional hearing materials include transcripts from the proceedings and documents such as prepared testimony and exhibits.

Floor debates are published in the *Congressional Record*. Be wary in relying on these debates as they may not have actually been delivered in the House or Senate; members of Congress can amend their remarks and even submit written statements that are published in transcript form as if they were spoken.

B. Compiled Legislative History

Some researchers have compiled legislative histories for certain federal statutes. A widely known reference book that compiles legislative histories of major federal statues is *Sources of Compiled Legislative Histories*.[17]

C. Online Sources for Federal Legislative History

LexisNexis and Westlaw have legislative history databases covering laws on a variety of topics, including the environment, bankruptcy, securities, immigration, and tax. Both services offer full-text sources. Examples include:

- LexisNexis
  - CERCLA Legislative History
  - Financial Institutions Reform, Recovery Enforcement Act of 1989
  - Tax Legislative Histories, Combined
- Westlaw
  - Americans with Disabilities Act
  - Bankruptcy Reform Act of 1994
  - Sarbanes-Oxley Act of 2002

---

17. Nancy P. Johnson, *Sourced of Compiled Legislative Histories: A Bibliography of Government Documents, Periodical Articles, and Books* (AALL 1979–present) (also available at www.heinonline.org).

Hein Online contains a *Legislative History Library* with a collection of fifteen compiled legislative histories. Examples include:

- Administrative Procedure Act
- Americans with Disabilities Act of 1990
- Civil Rights Act of 1991
- Copyright Act of 1909

Chapter 9

Administrative Law

I. Administrative Law and Governmental Agencies

Administrative law encompasses the rules and decisions of governmental agencies. Agencies include officers, departments, bureaus, divisions, boards, authorities, or commissions that are "authorized by law to administer, enforce, or interpret any law of this state."[1]

The term "state agency" refers to the executive branch of the State of Kansas, but does "not include any political or taxing subdivision of the state, or any agency thereof, or the judicial or legislative branch of state government."[2] The statutory or constitutional provisions that create agencies establish the powers and duties of the agencies. Each agency must work within the limits set by its enabling statute or constitutional provision.

Administrative law is primary authority like statutes and cases. It is unique because agencies perform functions of all three branches of government. Agencies write rules that interpret and apply statutes in the agencies' jurisdictions; these rules are similar in form and in authority to statutes enacted by the legislature. As part of the executive branch, agencies issue licenses (such as those permitting citizens to drive) and conduct investigations to see whether laws are being fol-

---

1. K.S.A. 77-602.
2. K.S.A. 77-602(k).

lowed (e.g., inspecting environmental sites). Agencies also hold quasi-judicial hearings, deciding cases that involve the agency's rules or its mission (e.g., to suspend a dental license or award unemployment benefits). These hearings are similar to court proceedings, but less formal.

The Kansas Administrative Procedures Act (KAPA)[3] was passed in 1984, became effective on July 1, 1985, and is codified in the Kansas statutes at KSA 77-501 et seq. The main objective of KAPA is to ensure a fair and impartial hearing for a person who contests a state agency action that has impacted the person's legal rights. In Kansas, due to the definitional limitations imposed by the legislature,[4] portions of major agency activities and functions are not covered by the KAPA. What this means for the researcher is that, in Kansas, it is necessary for you to check the enabling act not only of each agency you are dealing with, but also of the particular function of the agency you are researching. The KAPA will be applicable only if referenced.[5] A huge help for the researcher in Kansas is enabling act amendments, which incorporate all or part of the following state regulatory functions, listed in Table 9-1, within the KAPA.

II. Administrative Rules

Administrative agencies promulgate *rules*, similar to the legislature enacting statutes. Administrative rules are written in an outline-numbering format similar to that of statutes. Rules are defined by Kansas statute to include "a standard, statement of policy or general order, including amendments or revocations thereof, of general application and having the effect of law, issued or adopted by a state agency to implement or interpret legislation enforced or administered by such state agency or to govern the organization or procedure of such state agency. Every rule and regulation adopted

---

3. K.S.A. 77-501 et seq.
4. David L. Ryan, *The New Kansas Administrative and Judicial Review Acts*, J. Kan. B. Assn., Spring 1985, at 54–56.
5. *Id.*

Table 9-1. Kansas Regulatory Functions with the KAPA

Abstracters	Optometry
Accountants	Pest Control
Adult Care Homes	Pharmacy
Air Quality Control Board	Physical Therapists
Ambulance Service Operators	Podiatry
Barbers	Private Investigators
Cosmetology	Psychologists
Dental	Public Livestock Markets
Embalmers	Real Estate Salesman/Brokers
Healing Arts Board	Securities Brokers
Hearing Aids Technicians	Social Workers
Hospitals	Technical Professions
Insurance Agents	Vehicle Distributors/Dealers
Lodging and Food Service	Veterinarians
Maternity Hospitals/Homes	Veterinary Examiners
Medical Clinics	Water System and Waste
Mental Health Technicians	Water Treatment Operators
Nursing	Water Well Contractors
	Weather Modification Projects

Source: David L. Ryan, *The New Kansas Administrative and Judicial Review Acts*, J. Kan. B. Assn., Spring 1985, at 56–57.

by a state agency to govern its enforcement or administration of legislation shall be adopted by the state agency and filed as a rule and regulation."[6]

Administrative rules and regulations of the various state agencies are arranged in accordance with a three-part system of numbers divided by hyphens. The first number indicates the agency; the second number indicates the article (a group of regulations of that agency on the same subject); the last number indicates the specific section or regulation within the article. For example, "102-3-5a" refers to the Behavioral Science Regulatory Board, article on professional counsel, and section on examinations.

---

6. K.S.A. 77-415(4).

Table 9-2. Outline for Kansas Administrative Law Research

---

1. Find the statutory or constitutional provision granting the agency power to act. Research case law to determine whether the agency acted within that power.
2. Find the text of the relevant rule in *Kansas Administrative Regulations* (KAR) for the year at issue.
3. Update the rule in the *Kansas Register* to find any proposed changes.
4. Find agency and judicial decisions applying the rule in similar circumstances.

The law requires that agencies cite the statutory authority for the regulation and the section(s) of the statutes that the regulation implements. This is published at the end of the text of the regulation. In addition, the secretary of state includes a history of the regulation that indicates the original effective date of the regulation and each subsequent amendment.[7]

III. Researching Kansas Administrative Law

The basic process for researching Kansas administrative law is outlined in Table 9-2 and explained below.

A. Researching the Enabling Act

Analytically, the initial question with any agency action is whether the agency acted within its power. If that is in doubt, the first step in researching an administrative rule is to find the enabling provision (statutory or constitutional) that gives the agency power to act. The next step is to find cases that interpret the statute's provisions. Chapters 2 and 7 explain the process of researching constitutional provisions and statutes,

---

7. *Kansas Administrative Regulations* (KAR), Explanatory Preface (2007).

respectively. Chapters 4 and 5 explain how to find cases in addition to those listed in annotated codes. If the agency's power is clear, skip this inquiry and move directly to finding relevant rules, as explained next.

B. *Kansas Administrative Regulations*

Kansas's permanent rules are published annually by the Kansas Secretary of State in *Kansas Administrative Regulations* (known as KAR). The KAR volumes are updated with an annual cumulative supplement and subject index. It is published after December 31 of the preceding year and distributed in July or August of the current year.

EXAMPLE: The 2006 KAR contained all permanent rules and regulations filed before January 1, 2006. The 2007 cumulative supplement index contained rules and regulations filed after December 2005 and before January 1, 2007.[8]

Kansas administrative rules and regulations are available on the Kansas Legislature website at www.kslegislature.org/legsrv-kars/index.do. You can search for specific regulations on this site by regulation citation or keyword. The KARs are updated through January 1 of the preceding year. To find newer administrative regulations, view the *Kansas Register* online on the Kansas Secretary of State website at www.kssos.org/pubs/pubs_kansas_register.asp or contact the agency enacting the regulation. There is no lag time for the weekly *Kansas Register* on the Kansas Secretary of State website.

Kansas administrative rules are also available on both Westlaw and LexisNexis under the Kansas tabs. Both services allow searching either the full text of the rules or the KAR table of contents. On Westlaw and LexisNexis, there can be a currency lag time of several weeks. To search previous versions of KAR, Westlaw provides archival material dating from 2000, while LexisNexis coverage dates back to 2004. To find links to the archival material on Westlaw, you will need to

---

8. *Id.*

navigate from the "Directory" tab, which is not obviously visible from the list of links located at the very top of the page.

After finding relevant rules, read the text of each rule carefully. Many techniques used for reading statutes apply equally well to reading administrative rules.[9] In particular, always look for a separate rule that provides definitions, be aware of cross-references, read the text several times, and outline any complicated provisions. Figure 9-3 provides an example of a Kansas rule.

Following the text of each rule is the history of that rule. The history at the end of each regulation cites the authorizing and implementing statute(s). Taking the example from Figure 9-3, the history starts at the end of the regulation with the language; "as amended by L. 1999, Ch. 117, Sec. 8; effective Dec. 19, 1997; amended Aug. 4, 2000."

A permanent regulation is effective 15 days following its publication in the *Kansas Register* or at a later date specified in the body of the regulation. Prior to July 1, 1995, a permanent regulation became effective 45 days following publication in the *Kansas Register* or at a later date specified in the body of the regulation. The regulation remains in effect until amended or revoked.[10]

Temporary regulations have a slightly different history line. For example, in "amended, T-7-12-11-90, Dec. 31, 1990" the "T" means temporary, the "7" is the number assigned to the agency in the KAR volumes, and 12-11-90 is the date that the regulation was filed. Following the last comma is the effective date. Therefore, the amendment was filed as a temporary regulation on December 11, 1990, and the amendment became effective on December 31, 1990. If the "T number" is not included in an action on a regulation, the regulation was filed as a permanent regulation. A temporary regulation becomes effective upon approval by the States Rules and Regulations Board and filing in the Kansas Secretary of State's Office or at a later date when specified in the body of the regulation. A temporary regulation lasts 120 days unless it is amended or revoked within 120 days.

---

9. *See* Chapter 7, § I.A.3.

10. This language is found in the KAR commentary material in the front of each volume.

Figure 9-3. Example of a Kansas Rule

Kansas Administrative Regulations
Agency 102. Behavioral Sciences Regulatory Board
Article 3. Professional Counselors

102-3-5a Examinations

(a)(1) An Applicant for licensure as a professional counselor shall take a nationally administered, standardized written examination approved by the board. The minimum passing score shall be the criterion-referenced cutoff score.

(2) The applicant's required written examination may be waived by the board if the applicant has successfully passed a nationally administered, standardized written examination deemed by the board to be substantially equivalent to the examination used in this state and if the applicant obtained a score equal to or greater than the criterion-referenced cutoff score.

(3) An applicant shall not be authorized to register for the examination or to qualify for a waiver of the examination until the applicant has fulfilled all educational requirements and has satisfied the board that the applicant merits the public trust.

(Authorized by the KSA 1999 Supp. 74-7507; implementing KSA 1999 Supp. 65-5804, as amended by L. 1999, Ch. 117, Sec. 8; effective Dec. 19, 1997; amended Aug. 4, 2000.)

KAR 102-3-5a, KS ADC 102-3-5a

KS ADC 102-3-5a

Source: *Kansas Administrative Regulations*, § 102-3-5a (2006).

C. *Kansas Register*

Updates to Kansas rules are published weekly by the secretary of state in the *Kansas Register*. The *Register* is available both in print and online through the secretary of state's website. The website contains the current issue of the *Register* as well as past issues from recent years. The *Register* is available on LexisNexis under the Kansas tab retrospective to 1999. Although Westlaw does not contain the *Register* itself, updates are incorporated into Westlaw's database of *Kansas Administrative Regulations.*

To find the most recent version of a regulation, first check the index in the *Kansas Register*, next check the current KAR Supplement, and finally check the current KAR volume. *If the regulation is found at any of these sequential steps, stop and consider that version the most recent.* For example, the 2006 volumes replaced the 2003 volumes. At printing, the current publication consists of all six volumes of the 2006 *Kansas Administrative Regulations* with a one-volume 2007 Supplement. Regulations filed after December 31, 2007, can be found by using the *Kansas Register*'s index to the KAR. When an individual volume is published, it replaces the same volume of an earlier year. For example, a 2006 volume 2 would replace a 2003 volume 2.[11]

Being the official newspaper of Kansas, the *Kansas Register* contains more than just updates to the KARs. In addition to full text of newly adopted administrative regulations, the *Kansas Register* contains:

- Notices of hearings on proposed administrative regulations of state agencies.
- Notices of meetings of legislative interim committees.
- Hearing dockets of the Kansas Supreme Court and Court of Appeals.
- Any legislative bills that have been introduced.
- Monthly lists of forfeited corporations.
- Summaries of attorney general opinions.
- Notices of municipal bond values/redemptions.
- Invitations for bids/requests for proposals and many other legal and public notices/announcements.

D. Agency Decisions

What happens if there is a disagreement as to the application of the various agency rules published in the *Kansas Administrative Regulations*? If the disagreement cannot be resolved, it may be adjudi-

---

11. *Id.*

cated in a hearing before an administrative law judge. In Kansas, agencies are authorized to conduct hearings under the Kansas Administrative Procedure Act (KAPA). However, there is no statutory requirement in KAPA that directs the various agencies to publish their decisions or orders. KAPA does require that agencies keep their documents on hand for any possible public inspection.

Some commercial publishers have picked up the task of publishing the various agency opinions. One caveat: the agencies themselves are the final authority regardless of what a commercial publisher states. See *Kansas Legal Research and Reference Guide, 3d Edition*, Chapter 7 for where to find various Kansas agency decisions or orders.[12]

Previous hearing outcomes are not binding as precedent in administrative hearings. However, they can be very persuasive. They can help researchers mold arguments.

IV. Attorney General Opinions

The opinions of the Kansas Attorney General have the characteristics of both primary and secondary authority. As the legal advisor to the executive officials of the government, the attorney general renders requested legal advice to them, generally in the form of written opinions. Although these opinions are the official statements of an executive officer, issued in accordance with his/her authority, they are merely advisory statements and not mandatory orders. Therefore, the inquirers and other officials are not bound to follow the recommendations and conclusions. However, the opinions are persuasive and are generally followed by executive officers and city and county officials who request opinions. The opinions relate to general legal problems and interpret state statutes. The Kansas Attorney General issues advisory opinions on the interpretation of statutes and on the constitutionality of bills and ordinances to state

---

12. *Kansas Legal Research and Reference Guide, 3d Edition* (Joseph Custer ed., KBA Pub. 2003).

executive officials, to local prosecutors, and to legislators. (The attorney general conducts separate reviews on legislation prior to passage and before the governor signs it.)

Volumes containing the full opinions of the attorney general from 1957 to 1974 are available in most depository libraries. From 1975, only digests of the opinions have been distributed.[13] Full opinions since 1975 are available at the Supreme Court Law Library in Topeka, the University of Kansas Wheat Law Library and the attorney general's office. Washburn University Law Library has full opinions in print since 1980. Kansas attorney general opinions are available on LexisNexis and Westlaw since 1977. This is particularly useful because it is possible to find desired opinions simply by searching for opinions containing certain words, phrases, or statutes. Generally, however, to find which attorney general opinions over the years, if any, have been issued on any particular statute, the simplest thing to do is call the attorney general's office in Topeka. Attorney general opinions are now available free of charge via the Washburn Law School website retrospective to 1993 at http://ksag.washburnlaw.edu.

V. Federal Administrative Law

The federal government's agencies function much like Kansas's agencies. The Civil Rights Division of the Department of Justice, the Internal Revenue Service, and the U.S. Fish and Wildlife Service are invaluable parts of the executive branch.

The Federal APA is codified at 5 USC § 551 et seq. Like Kansas's APA, its goals are to promote uniformity, public participation, and public confidence in the fairness of the procedures used by agencies of the federal government.

---

13. There is a table of statutes for each bound volume beginning with 1957. For opinions before 1957, the attorney general's office must be contacted directly.

Figure 9-4. Example of a Federal Regulation

36 CFR 223.2

TITLE 36–PARKS, FORESTS, AND PUBLIC PROPERTY
CHAPTER 11–FOREST SERVICE, DEPARTMENT OF AGRICULTURE
PART 223–SALE AND DISPOSAL OF NATIONAL FOREST SYSTEM
TIMBER
Subpart A–General Provisions
Sec. 223.2 Disposal of timber for administrative use.

Trees, portions of trees, or other forest products in any amount on National Forest System lands may be disposed of for administrative use, by sale or without charge, as may be most advantageous to the United States, subject to the maximum cut fixed in accordance with established policies for management of the National Forests. Such administrative use shall be limited to the following conditions and purposes:
(a) For construction, maintenance or repair of roads, bridges, trails, telephone lines, fences, recreation areas or other improvements of value for the protection or the administration of Federal lands.
(b) For fuel in Federal camps, buildings and recreation areas.
(c) For research and demonstration projects.
(d) For use in disaster relief work conducted by public agencies.
(e) For disposal when removal is desirable to protect or enhance multiple-use values in a particular area.

Source: *Code of Federal Regulations*, volume 36, chapter 11, page 80 (2007).

A. *Code of Federal Regulations*

Federal administrative rules are called *regulations*. Federal regulations are published by the Government Printing Office (GPO) in the *Code of Federal Regulations* (CFR).

Similar to KAR in Kansas, regulations in CFR are organized by agency and subject. The fifty titles of CFR do not necessarily correspond to the fifty titles of the *United States Code* (USC), although some topics do fall under the same title number. For instance, Title 7 in both CFR and USC pertain to agriculture, but Title 11 of USC addresses bankruptcy, while the same title in CFR deals with federal elections. See Figure 9-4 for an example of a federal regulation.

CFR volumes are updated annually, with specific titles updated each quarter. Titles 1 through 16 are updated as of January 1;[14] titles 17 through 27 are updated as of April 1; titles 28 through 41 are updated as of July 1; and titles 42 through 50 are updated as of October 1. Realize, though, that the updates may only become available months after the schedule indicates. Each year, the covers of CFR volumes are a different color, which makes it easy to tell whether a print volume has been updated. If no changes were made in a particular volume for the new year, a cover with the new color is pasted on the old volume.

To research a topic in CFR, you may use the general index. Look up your research terms or the relevant agency's name, and then read the regulations referenced. It may be more efficient to begin your research in an annotated statutory code that contains references to related regulations for each statute. After finding a statute on point, review the annotations following the statutory language for cross-references to relevant regulations; you may notice that *United States Code Service* tends to provide more references to regulations than does *United States Code Annotated*. Look up the citations given and review the regulations.

Federal regulations are available online at www.gpoaccess.gov/cfr. The text there is no more current than the print versions, but searching may be preferred by those skilled in online research. The site allows searching by keyword, citation, and title.

CFR is also available on LexisNexis and Westlaw. The code is kept current by these services, eliminating the need for updating, which is explained below.

B. *Federal Register*

New regulations and proposed changes to existing regulations are published first in the *Federal Register*, the federal equivalent to the *Kansas Register*. The *Federal Register* is the first print source to pub-

---

14. The exception is title 3, "The President," which includes executive orders. Unlike other CFR titles, it is not updated annually.

lish regulations in their final form when they are adopted (i.e., before they are codified in CFR). In addition to providing the text of regulations, the *Federal Register* also contains notices of hearings, responses to public comments on proposed regulations, and helpful tables and indexes. It is published almost every weekday, with continuous pagination throughout the year. This means that page numbers in the thousands are common. The online version of the *Federal Register* is available at www.gpoaccess.gov/fr. The *Federal Register* is also available on LexisNexis and Westlaw.

C. Updating a Federal Regulation

To update a federal regulation in print or on the government's website, begin with a small booklet or the database called *List of CFR Sections Affect* (LSA). As its name suggests, LSA lists all sections of CFR that have been affected by recent agency action. LSA provides page references to *Federal Register* issues where action affecting a section of CFR is included. If the section you are researching is not listed in LSA, then it has not been changed since its annual revision. LSA is published monthly and is available online at www.gpoaccess.gov/lsa.

Final updating requires reference to a table at the back of the *Federal Register* called "CFR Parts Affected During [the current month]." (Do not confuse this table with the "CFR Parts Affected in this [Current] Issue" located in the Contents at the beginning of each issue.) Refer to this table in each *Federal Register* for the last day of each month for all the months between the most recent monthly LSA issue and the current date. Also check the most recent issue of *Federal Register* for the present month. The table contains more general information (whether a "part" has been affected, not a "section"), but will note changes made since the most recent monthly LSA. CFR Parts Affected is available online through a link on the LSA website noted above.

The updating described above is similar to using pocket parts to update research in a digest. Federal regulations can be Shepardized on LexisNexis and can be updated with KeyCite on Westlaw.

D. Decisions of Federal Agencies

Like Kansas agencies, federal agencies hold quasi-judicial hearings to decide cases that arise under the agencies' regulations. Some of these decisions are published in reporters specific to each agency, for example, *Decisions and Orders of the National Labor Relations Board* (NLRB). Increasingly, agency decisions are available on agency websites and from LexisNexis and Westlaw.

E. Judicial Opinions

The methods of case research explained in Chapters 4 and 5 will lead to opinions in which the judiciary reviewed decisions of federal agencies. Additionally, *Shepard's Code of Federal Regulations Citations* is a useful research tool both for updating federal regulations and for finding cases relevant to regulatory research. Shepard's is available on LexisNexis; the Westlaw counterpart is KeyCite. Both are explained in Chapter 6 of this book.

Chapter 10

Legal Ethics Research

I. Introduction

It's hard to imagine any practicing Kansas attorney not ever coming into contact with a legal ethics issue to research. Some examples are duties owed to former clients, exceptions to the attorney-client privilege, and authority given to legal assistants to conduct the duties of a lawyer.

This type of research will often involve gray areas and close calls. It involves matters with high stakes, affecting the lawyer's reputation in addition to the basic right to practice.

Researching a Kansas legal ethics issue may include referring to resources from jurisdictions outside Kansas. Kansas will typically consider other jurisdictions' precedents if there is not enough within its own. Legal research ethics sources, such as the American Bar Association (ABA) resources, are considered a nationwide equivalent to Kansas Bar Association (KBA) resources and can be persuasive when Kansas precedent is lacking. Other states' law may also be looked at.

II. The Model Rules: A Brief History

The ABA released the *Canons of Professional Ethics* in 1908 based on the Alabama Bar Association's *Code of Ethics*. In 1969, the ABA adopted the *Model Code of Professional Responsibility* (Model Code). In 1983, the ABA adopted the *Model Rules of Professional Conduct* (Model

Table 10-1. Historical Timeline of United States
Rules of Professional Ethics

1836	David Hoffman, founder of University of Maryland Law School, wrote fifty *Resolutions in Regard to Professional Development* for his students.
1854	Honorable George Sharswood, professor of law at University of Pennsylvania, published *A Compend[ium] of Lectures on the Aims and Duties of the Profession of Law.*
1887	David Goode Jones, an Alabama attorney, provided leadership that led to the adoption of the *Code of Ethics* by the Alabama Bar Association.
1908	The American Bar Association adopted the *Canons of Professional Ethics* based on the Alabama Bar Association's *Code of Ethics.*
1969	The Special Committee on Evaluation of Ethical Standards produced, and the ABA adopted, the *Model Code of Professional Responsibility* (Model Code).
1977	The ABA Commission on Evaluation of Professional Standards (Kutak Commission) was formed.
1983	The ABA House of Delegates adopted the *Model Rules of Professional Conduct* (Model Rules).
1997	The ABA's Ethics 2000 Commission began writing new rules to address current issues; subsequently, most remaining Model Code states adopted all or part of the Model Rules.

Source: *Georgia Legal Research* (Carolina Academic Press 2007).

Rules). The Model Rules have been revised several times since. The various versions of ethical rules the ABA has adopted are depicted in Table 10-1.

The ABA Model Rules are intended to serve as a national framework for implementation of standards of professional conduct. The Model Rules, like all model legislation, are subject to state adoption, implementation, and modification. The Model Rules were adopted and approved by the Kansas Supreme Court in 1988. The rules became effective in 1989 and are called the *Kansas Rules of Professional Conduct* (KRPC). They vary only slightly from the ABA Model Rules.

Table 10-2. Legal Ethics Research Steps

Step 1	List the parties involved.
Step 2	List the issues in keyword or short phrase form.
Step 3	List all jurisdictions that could apply to your research problem.
Step 4	Search Kansas rules and their equivalent counterparts.
Step 5	Search Kansas case law and its equivalent counterparts.
Step 6	Assess whether your research is complete. If not, proceed to Step 7.
Step 7	Seek resources from the ABA; if none exist, seek resources from other states as last resort precedent.
Step 8	Consult relevant secondary sources.

III. The Research Process

In researching a legal ethics issue, various primary and secondary resources must be pulled together. A checklist in Table 10-2 helps organize the research steps.

A. Beginning the Research

First, list the parties involved, e.g., current counsel, past counsel, legal assistants, supervisors. Next, identify all the legal issues involved and formulate keywords or short phrases, which will be used to research print indexes or online databases. More often than not, legal ethics research focuses on the state level. List the state jurisdictions that could apply.

B. Finding Kansas Rules

The *Kansas Rules of Professional Conduct* (KRPC) are found at Kansas Supreme Court Rule 226 et seq. Several print sources contain the KPRC, including *ABA/BNA Lawyer's Manual on Professional Conduct, Kansas Court Rules and Procedure, State and Federal,*[1] and the

---

1. This is a Thomson/West publication.

Rules Adopted by the Supreme Court of the State of Kansas Annotated.[2] The KRPC are available from the Kansas Judicial Center in Topeka, Kansas. A free online source for the KRPC is the Kansas Judicial site at www.kscourts.org/rules.

Separate rules exist to govern judicial conduct in Kansas. The Kansas Code of Judicial Conduct is Rule 601 et seq. of the Kansas Rules Relating to Judicial Conduct. The Rules Relating to Judicial Conduct are available in *Rules Enacted by the Supreme Court of the State of Kansas Annotated* and also in *Kansas Court Rules and Procedure, State and Federal.* The Rules Relating to Judicial Conduct are also available for free online at www.kscourts.org/rules/Rule-List.asp?r1=Rules+Relating+to+Judicial+Conduct.

After locating relevant rules, seek relevant Kansas statutes. In the majority of situations, there will not be a statute on point. For thorough research, however, it is necessary to search the statutes.

C. Researching Kansas Case Law and its Legal Ethics Counterparts

Step 5 in Table 10-2 states to seek Kansas case law and its legal ethic counterparts, such as Kansas advisory opinions, disciplinary proceedings, and other documents that may have precedential value.

1. Kansas Case Law

Relevant Kansas case law may be a useful resource if Kansas courts have interpreted or applied ethics rules relevant to your research. To locate cases you can either use a print or online digest or a case law database. Refer back to Chapter 5 for the process of doing case law research.

One note on analyzing Kansas case law and the current standards: The case law may look the same as the current standard but indeed may be different depending on the context. Courts' attitudes over the

---

2. This is a Kansas Supreme Court publication.

years in Kansas have changed regarding professional responsibility. Some of this is due to a change in the rules governing professional conduct, but by and large it is in regard to changes that have occurred over the years in the practice of law, just as in any other area of law (i.e., attorney advertising).

2. *Judicial Ethics Advisory Opinions*

A judicial ethics advisory panel, consisting of no more than three retired justices or judges serving at the pleasure of the Kansas Supreme Court, sits as an advisory committee for judges seeking opinions concerning the compliance of an intended, future course of conduct with the Code of Judicial Conduct.[3]

Advisory opinions address only whether an intended, future course of conduct violates the Code of Judicial Conduct and provide an interpretation of the code with regard to the factual situation presented.[4] The opinions do not address issues of law, nor do they address the ethical priority of past or present conduct. The identity of the requesting judge is not to be disclosed in the opinion. The advisory opinion is not binding on the Supreme Court in the exercise of its judicial discipline responsibilities.[5]

3. *KBA Ethics Advisory Opinions*

The Kansas Bar Association (KBA) Ethics Advisory Opinions are available through the online legal database Casemaker to members of the KBA. A member of the Kansas Bar Association, by using his or her ID number and password, can gain access to all ethics opinions retrospective to 1988 on the Kansas Bar Association website through Casemaker (www.ksbar.org/casemaker). Ethics advisory opinions are also available to everyone on the Kansas Judicial Branch website.[6]

---

3. Rule 650 Relating to Judicial Conduct.
4. Rule 650, *supra* n. 3.
5. *Id.*
6. The web address is www.kscourts.org/appellate-clerk/general/judicial-ethics.asp.

Ethics opinions are not issued if the matter on which an opinion is being sought is the subject of litigation. Requests must concern a lawyer's own future conduct. Opinions are also not issued with regard to questions of law, such as interpretations of rules, statutes, or cases. The Office of Disciplinary Administrator will frequently discuss ethical situations with attorneys and this might be where an attorney should make a first inquiry, especially in situations where time is running short.

4. Disciplinary Cases

Complaints against attorneys are investigated by local bar associations or the Disciplinary Administrator's staff, who may seek further information.[7] Many complaints are resolved or dismissed after preliminary investigation. Once the investigation is complete, a review committee consisting of three lawyers is assigned to study the complaint and investigate the report. The committee may then dismiss the complaint if it is found to be without merit.

If the review committee finds probable cause to believe the lawyer has violated the disciplinary rules, the matter becomes public and all records and proceedings are open to anyone. The review committee may informally admonish the lawyer or, if stronger discipline appears warranted, the committee may direct the Disciplinary Administrator to prepare a formal complaint. The lawyer is normally given twenty days to respond to the complaint before a hearing is scheduled.

The hearing panel consists of three lawyers, including at least two members of the Kansas Board for Discipline of Attorneys. The Disciplinary Administrator's Office presents evidence in support of the formal complaint. The accused lawyer is entitled to representation by counsel and may present witnesses and evidence in defense. The complainant may be required to testify at this hearing.

The hearing panel may find that no violation of the disciplinary rules occurred, or it may determine that a minor violation occurred

---

7. Descriptions in this section are taken from the website of the Kansas Judicial Branch Office of Disciplinary Administration at www.kscourts.org/ Rules_Procedures_Forms/Attorney_Discipline/complaints.asp.

as a result of a mistake rather than an intentional act and may impose an informal admonition. In that case the lawyer is summoned before the Disciplinary Administrator, admonished about the violation, and warned not to repeat the conduct.

If the hearing panel finds that a violation occurred and more serious discipline is warranted, the panel submits to the Kansas Supreme Court a formal report setting forth its factual and legal findings and making recommendations for discipline of the lawyer. Recommended discipline could be public censure, probation with conditions, suspension of the lawyer's license for a specific time period, suspension for an indefinite period, or disbarment.[8]

Discipline cases submitted to the Kansas Supreme Court are processed in much the same way as any other appellate case, with both sides entitled to present written and oral arguments. In addition, the Supreme Court reviews a transcript of the proceedings before the hearing panel.

The Supreme Court need not follow the recommendations of the hearing panel or the Disciplinary Administrator. The Court may determine that no violation occurred, or it may impose a different form of discipline from that recommended by the hearing panel.

An excellent free online source to search for published Kansas Supreme Court Disciplinary Cases is the office of the Kansas Disciplinary Administrator site at www.kscourts.org/rules-procedures-forms/attorney-discipline/default.asp.

D. Locating Precedent from Other Jurisdictions and Secondary Sources

In Step 6, you consider whether your research is complete. Your research is complete if you have enough Kansas sources to address your ethics issue. Steps 7 and 8 are optional and should be explored if your research is not complete at this point. If your research does not seem complete, try the following sources.

---

8. Rule 650, *supra* n. 3.

Precedent from other jurisdictions may hold weight in Kansas courts when Kansas precedent is lacking. Using your keywords, consult statutory and case law resources and their counterparts from the ABA.

Secondary sources are another excellent source. Consult resources such as the *ABA/BNA Lawyer's Manual on Professional Conduct*; the *Restatement of the Law, the Law Governing Lawyers*; law review articles; and other sources of commentary.

A very helpful secondary resource is the *ABA/BNA Lawyer's Manual on Professional Conduct*. It contains the full text of both the Model Codes and the Rules. It contains digests of state ethics opinions also. It has a topical discussion of the Model Code and Rules with state variations. You can identify the ABA model and compare Kansas variations. Another advantage to using this resource is that you can identify standards from other states and see how they correspond to Kansas rules.

Another important secondary source is the *Restatement of the Law, the Law Governing Lawyers*.[9] The form of the publication follows that of other restatements with black-letter standards accompanied by comments, illustrations, and reporter's notes. The notes section can be a great resource for further research. There are also helpful tables of codes and cases, rules, standards, cross-references to the West Digest system, *American Law Reports*, and a fine index. The *Restatement* is available on LexisNexis and Westlaw.

Another outstanding source for legal ethics research and a potential mother lode of footnotes is the legal periodical. A thoughtful query in the *Index to Legal Periodicals* or the *Current Law Index* on professional responsibility or legal ethics will almost always obtain research results. Both of these indexes are also available online through LexisNexis or Westlaw. Specialized periodicals are of particular note, including the *Georgetown Journal of Legal Ethics*, the University of Alabama's *Journal of Legal Profession*, and the *Notre Dame Journal of Law Ethics and Public Policy*.

---

9. This is an American Law Institute publication.

Appendix 10-A. Sources of Kansas Rules of Professional Conduct (KRPC) Online

BUREAU OF NATIONAL AFFAIRS (BNA)—Commercial www.bna.com	
Content	*ABA/BNA Lawyer's Manual on Professional Conduct*
Coverage	Current version of KRPC
Update	Updated as received from the Kansas Supreme Court

KANSAS JUDICIAL—Free www.kscourts.org/rules	
Content	*Kansas Rules of Professional Conduct*
Coverage	Current version of KRPC
Update	Updated as received from the Kansas Supreme Court

LEXISNEXIS—Commercial www.lexis.com	
Content	*Kansas Rules of Professional Conduct*
Coverage	Current version of KRPC
Update	Updated as received from the Kansas Supreme Court

LOISLAW—Commercial www.loislaw.com	
Content	*Kansas Rules of Professional Conduct*
Coverage	Current version of KRPC
Update	Updated as received from the Kansas Supreme Court

WESTLAW—Commercial www.westlaw.com	
Content	*Kansas Rules of Professional Conduct*
Coverage	Current version of KRPC
Update	Updated as received from the Kansas Supreme Court

Appendix 10-B. Sources of Ethics Cases, Advisory Opinions, and Disciplinary Proceedings Online

CASEMAKER — Bar Members www.ksbar.org/casemaker	
Content	Kansas ethics opinions
Coverage	1988–current
Update	Updated as issued by the Kansas Supreme Court

KANSAS DISCIPLINARY ADMINISTRATOR — Free www.kscourts.org/rules-procedures-forms/attorney-discipline/default.asp	
Content	Kansas disciplinary cases
Coverage	October 25, 1996 to present
Update	Updated as issued by the Kansas Supreme Court

LEXISNEXIS — Commercial www.lexis.com	
Content	Kansas legal ethics and professional responsibility cases
Coverage	1862 to present
Update	Updated as issued by the Supreme Court and Court of Appeals of Kansas

LEXISNEXIS — Commercial www.lexis.com	
Content	*National Reporter on Legal Ethics and Professional Responsibility*
Coverage	Selected formal and informal ethics opinions 1991–present
Update	Monthly
Notes	Database includes all fifty states; limit to Kansas by using the following segment search: STATE (Kansas)

WESTLAW — Commercial www.westlaw.com	
Content	Kansas legal ethics and professional responsibility cases
Coverage	1858 to present
Update	Updated as cases become available
Notes	Database is KSMAL-CS

Appendix 10-C. Precedent from Other Jurisdictions and Secondary Sources Online

AMERICAN BAR ASSOCIATION CENTER FOR PROFESSIONAL ETHICS—Free www.abanet.org/cpr/center_entities.html	
Content	Miscellaneous lawyer regulation resources
Coverage	Varies depending on the resource
Update	Schedule unknown
Notes	Contains the full text of the *Model Rules of Professional Conduct* available at www.abanet.org/cpr/mrpc/mrpc_home.html

LEXISNEXIS—Commercial www.lexis.com	
Content	*Restatement of the Law, the Law Governing Lawyers*
Coverage	Current restatement
Update	Updated regularly as received from publisher
Notes	LexisNexis features an Annotated Case Citations database that includes Annotations to Restatement Rules and Notes (updated annually) and the ALI's Interim Case Citations (updated two times per year)

NATIONAL ORGANIZATION OF BAR COUNSEL—Free http://nobc.org	
Content	Cases of the month—Featured disciplinary proceedings
Coverage	Selected disciplinary proceedings from all jurisdictions
Update	Monthly

WESTLAW—Commercial www.westlaw.com	
Content	Legal Ethics & Professional Responsibility—American Bar Association Ethics Opinions
Coverage	Formal opinions (January 1924-present) Informal opinions (July 1961-present)
Update	As new opinions are received from the ABA

Appendix 10-C. Precedent from Other Jurisdictions
and Secondary Sources Online, *continued*

	WESTLAW — Commercial www.westlaw.com
Content	*Restatement of the Law, the Law Governing Lawyers*
Coverage	Current restatement
Update	Three times per year
Notes	Westlaw also features a companion archive database that features all drafts of this restatement from Tentative Draft No.1, 1988, to the present

	WESTLAW — Commercial www.westlaw.com
Content	*ABA/BNA Lawyer's Manual on Professional Conduct*
Coverage	Current manual
Update	As the print manual is updated

Chapter 11

Online Legal Research

For most of the twentieth century, lawyers depended upon print publications for the preservation, organization, and dissemination of legal information. The relatively recent arrival of electronic alternatives has fundamentally altered this paradigm. Effective and cost-efficient legal research now necessitates fluency in online research methods. Unlike other online research, however, legal research requires a high level of precision, both in deciding where to search and in constructing searches.

This chapter begins with basic information for conducting legal research online. This introduction will be essential for researchers with less online experience, while providing a quick overview for researchers savvy about online techniques. The chapter then delves into more sophisticated search techniques. An appendix at the end of the chapter contains websites for finding Kansas law online.

Before delving into search strategies it is important to note that, despite the continuing evolution of sophisticated search engines, competent electronic legal research can rarely be reduced to a simple keyword search. This is because legal analysis is required at several crucial points in the research process. It is also because online legal resources are usually electronic transcriptions of intricate print publication systems with a hundred or more years of accumulated quirks and nuances. Because online resources often mirror print publications, other search techniques such as browsing tables of contents and using indexes remain vital components of an effective research strategy. That being said, keyword searching has most definitely become an indispensable implement in the modern legal researcher's toolbox. The ability of electronic databases to quickly scan thousands of sources allows the creation of customized lists of authority that were unimaginable in the old print paradigm.

Table 11-1. Outline for Constructing Terms and
Connectors Searches

1. Clarify the issue.
2. Choose a site or service.
3. Generate search terms, then modify them with expanders and
   placeholders.
4. Add connectors.
5. Refine the search based on the results.

I. Terms and Connectors Searching

One of the most common techniques for searching online databases is with terms and connectors. Also called Boolean searching,
this method uses connecting symbols to dictate where search terms
should be in relation to each other in the documents retrieved.[1] Terms
and connectors searches are typically conducted in the full text of
documents, looking for exact matches. An outline of the steps to constructing an effective search is provided in Table 11-1.

A. Clarify the Issue

First, carefully think through the legal issue. The importance of
this step cannot be overemphasized, as it lays the foundation for successful legal research—electronic or print. Review secondary sources,
clarify the relevant doctrine, note important facts, and identify terms
of art before running a search. Try to write a single sentence that
summarizes the question you hope to answer. Remember that the
computer is no smarter than you are, and it interprets Boolean
queries literally. A few minutes spent early in the research process developing a search query can save you hours of frustration and hundreds or thousands of dollars in wasted research expenses.

---

1. As noted in Chapter 1, George Boole was a British mathematician. The
Boolean connectors that carry his name dictate the logical relationship of
search terms to each other.

Table 11-2. Websites for Commercial Providers

Provider	Web Address
Casemaker (free to Kansas State Bar Members)	www.ksbar.org/casemaker
FindLaw (currently free)	www.findlaw.com
LexisNexis	www.lexis.com
LexisOne (currently free)	www.lexisone.com
Loislaw	www.loislaw.com
VersusLaw	www.versuslaw.com
Westlaw	www.westlaw.com

B. Choose a Site or Service

After clarifying the issue, determine which online sites you will use to conduct your search. Review the sites covered in Chapter 1, and consider whether the material you hope to find is available from a free, yet reliable, site. Weigh the cost of a commercial service like LexisNexis or Westlaw against their sophisticated search engines and vast resources. Table 11-2 lists the websites for some of the more common commercial providers.

After selecting an online provider, you must also choose which subset of that provider's resources to use. LexisNexis and Westlaw divide their resources into groups by type of document, topic, and jurisdiction. In LexisNexis, these groups are simply called *sources*. In Westlaw, information is grouped into *databases*, which is also the common generic term for such resource groups.

Both LexisNexis and Westlaw have directories to allow you to browse among the sources or databases that are available for research. Clicking on the "i" icon next to the name of a source will provide information about its scope. Note that the list of sources or databases shown on a particular page may not include all that are available. On LexisNexis, you may need to click on "View more sources." On Westlaw, you may need to view the "Directory."

Try to restrict each search to the smallest set of sources or databases that will contain the documents needed. Because online databases often correspond to print series, it may be helpful to think of yourself in the stacks of the library when choosing sources or databases. Do you really want to search the contents of every reporter on the third floor, or do you want to search just Kansas reporters? When looking for a constitutional provision, should you use a database that also contains statutes, legislative history, and court rules? In addition to producing a more focused set of results, smaller databases also tend to be less expensive than their larger counterparts.

C. Generate Search Terms

Generate a comprehensive list of search terms, following the suggestions in Chapter 1. This step is critically important in online research, given the literal nature of terms and connectors searching. If the author of a particular document does not use the exact term you are searching for, that document will not appear in your results. Both Westlaw and LexisNexis offer thesaurus-like features that suggest related terms for searches, but significant reliance upon these features may indicate a need to revisit Step 1 (Clarify the issue).

Most of the time, legal researchers are seeking authority that intersects their client's situation along two planes: 1) doctrine, and 2) facts. Therefore, a successful online search will usually include terms from both of these categories. Learning how to properly balance doctrine and facts in searches is a skill developed with time and practice. Before entering your search, consider whether elements of both categories are included. If either is lacking, you might need to further clarify the legal issue before proceeding.

In generating a list of terms, include both broad and narrow terms. For example, in a search specifically about medical malpractice, you may want to include the broader term *professional negligence*. Including synonyms and antonyms of search terms is sometimes necessary to conduct a thorough search. However, beware of the temptation to initially

Table 11-3. Example Queries

Goal	LexisNexis Query	Westlaw Query
Search for alternative terms	gun or firearm	gun firearm
Search for the phrase "standard of care"	standard of care	"standard of care"

construct unnecessarily complex searches. Balancing thoroughness and precision is a challenge that animates all keyword searching.

Sometimes it will be necessary to modify the search terms with expanders and placeholders so the search will find variations of your words. The exclamation point expands words beyond a common root. For example, *arbitrat!* will find arbitrate, arbitration, arbitrator, etc.

The asterisk serves as a placeholder for an individual letter. Up to three asterisks can be used in a single term. This symbol is helpful when you are not sure which form of the word is used, or when you are not sure of the spelling of a word. For example, the search term *dr*nk* will find drink, drank, and drunk. Place holders are preferable to the expander in some instances. Using an expander on *trad!* with hopes of finding trade, trading, trades, etc. will also produce results that include *traditional*. A better search term may be *trad*** .

D. Add Connectors

Connectors determine where search terms will be placed in relation to one another in targeted documents. Effective use of connectors is thus critical in finding relevant authority. Table 1-6 (in Chapter 1) summarizes the most common connectors used on LexisNexis and Westlaw.

Most connectors are the same for the two services. Two differences, however, can cause some confusion. On LexisNexis, searching alternative terms requires the use of the connector "or." On Westlaw, a blank space is interpreted as "or." The second difference concerns phrases or terms of art. LexisNexis reads a blank as joining words in a phrase. By contrast, to search a phrase on Westlaw, the terms must be enclosed in quotation marks. Examples are shown in Table 11-3.

Parentheses can be used to give priority to certain connectors. Even minimally sophisticated combinations of parentheses and the various connectors can make searches much more effective. Consider an example search designed to determine whether a contract containing a covenant not to compete is enforceable against a former employee.

> EXAMPLE: Searching terms: (covenant or contract) /p (noncompetition or "restraint of trade" or compet!) /p employ!, the computer will look for:
> - either the term *covenant* or *contract*
> - within the same paragraph as the term *noncompetition* or *restraint of trade* or variations of *competition, compete, competitor*
> - and also in that paragraph variations of *employ, employee, employer, employment.*

Misuse of connectors can produce bizarre search results. If, instead of "/p" in the example above, the researcher used the "or" connector, the results could include (1) a case in which former spies sued the federal government for failing to adhere to a secret *contract*, (2) a case determining whether an implied *covenant* can be read into an oil and gas lease, and (3) a case dismissing a beer importer's unfair *competition* claim.

E. Refine the Search

With a query of terms and connectors, you are ready to conduct a search. An initial search might locate either no documents or more than 1,000 documents. Boolean search results will typically be displayed in chronological order.

If a search produces no results, use broader connectors (e.g., search for terms in the same paragraph rather than in the same sentence), use additional alternative terms, or use a larger set of sources or a larger database. If a search produces a long list of results, skim them to see whether they are on point. If the results seem irrelevant, modify or edit the search query by omitting broad terms, using more restrictive connectors, or using a smaller set of sources or databases.

With practice, you will learn to craft more precise searches that produce more helpful results.

The "FOCUS" feature on LexisNexis and the "Locate" feature on Westlaw can be used to narrow results further. These features allow a researcher to construct a search within a search, and produce a subset of the initial search results. These features can be very cost efficient because they do not result in the additional charges of a new search. Indeed, a good strategy may be to create a broader initial search than you otherwise might and plan to conduct a series of restricting searches on the results.

II. Other Online Search Techniques

The text below introduces more sophisticated search techniques and offers suggestions for effective and efficient online research.

A. Segment and Field Searching

Both LexisNexis and Westlaw allow you to search specific parts of documents, such as the date, author, or court. The options are available on drop-down menus. On LexisNexis, these specific parts are called document *segments*; on Westlaw, they are called *fields*. A segment or field term is added to the basic search with an appropriate connector.

A few examples demonstrate the usefulness of segment and field searching. First, in conducting a full-text search, you can ensure that the results directly address your topic by searching the syllabi or synopses of the documents. Because this segment or field summarizes the contents of the document, your terms will appear there only if they are the focus of the document. Thus, the search will weed out documents where your terms are mentioned only in passing or in a footnote. Second, if you know the author of a relevant opinion or article, you can search for her name in the appropriate segment or field, eliminating documents where the person is referred to only tangentially.

B. Natural Language Searching

Natural language search engines allow searches that use a simple question or phrase, as opposed to a sometimes arcane series of terms and connectors. These search engines lack the precision of terms and connectors searching, but allow you to construct a search more quickly and intuitively. Natural language search engines employ proprietary algorithms designed to rank the relevance of the documents included in search results. Thus, this method of searching more closely resembles general Internet search engines such as Google.

The help natural language searching provides in ascertaining the value of search results can be a relief after the frustration of terms and connectors searches that returned no results, but several caveats are important. Although natural language formulas are continually improving, they cannot replace a human mind trained in the art of legal analysis. Sometimes the best hit from your perspective will be the search engine's fourteenth best match, so skimming through the results is always very important. Furthermore, natural language searching can sometimes produce entire lists of documents that are not very relevant to your research. This may mean that no better matches exist or that the search was not crafted well enough. On LexisNexis and Westlaw, the natural language programs are set to retrieve a particular number of results. Often the number is 20 or 100, though you can change the default. Again, the fact that the computer returned 100 documents does not mean that those 100 documents are all relevant. When conducting a search on the Internet, poor results may mean that this particular search engine did not scan the portion of the Internet that contains the needed documents.

While natural language searching can be very helpful to the novice online researcher, skilled terms and connectors searching will almost always be more powerful and accurate. Regardless of search type, legal analysis must drive the process—computers can provide information but they cannot answer legal questions. Law students should take advantage of their unfettered access to LexisNexis and Westlaw by extensively practicing both Boolean and natural language searching. Practitioners can take advantage of free training provided by the commercial providers.

C. Using Electronic Versions of Print Finding Aids

Many of the finding aids offered in print resources are also available online. In the realm of statutes, for example, Westlaw and LexisNexis replicate popular name tables for the USCA and USCS, respectively. Westlaw also offers an electronic version of the USCA General Index.

Recognizing that keyword searching is not always the solution for efficient research, online services are continually seeking to incorporate finding aids that were once available exclusively in print. One of the most common, and helpful, features is the table of contents option. This feature is especially useful when researching statutes and regulations. For example, LexisNexis displays the table of contents for the USCS upon entering the source. Clicking on the "+" icon next to a title will expand the table of contents to display chapters within that title, which can be further expanded to display sections. Figure 11-4 depicts this screen before any of the titles have been expanded. Westlaw offers a similar feature for the USCA that can be accessed by clicking on the "Table of Contents" link near the top of the page. Browsing tables of contents online is an important complement to keyword searching because viewing statutory sections in relation to their surroundings is often necessary to fully understand a given statute's meaning. Navigating labyrinthine statutory or regulatory codes is much simpler with a bit of context to guide the way.

There are also similar features that can be used to research case law. For example, Westlaw incorporates many features of the print *American Digest System*. Clicking on the "Key Numbers" link found at the top of the Westlaw screen leads to the "West Key Number Digest Out-

Figure 11-4. LexisNexis USCS Table of Contents

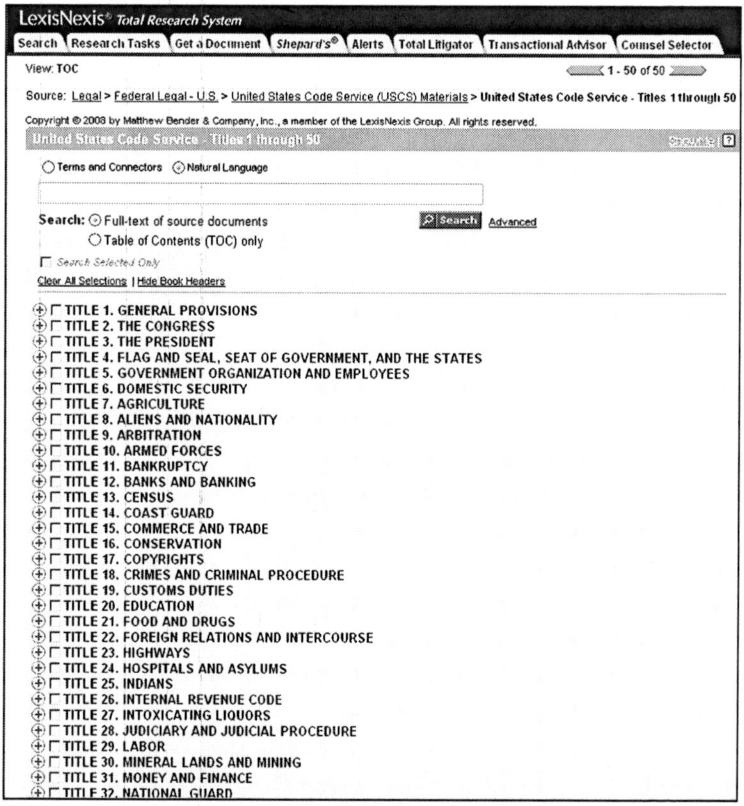

Source: LexisNexis. Copyright 2008 LexisNexis, a division of Reed Elsevier Inc. All Rights Reserved. LexisNexis and the Knowledge Burst logo are registered trademarks of Reed Elsevier Properties Inc. and are used with the permission of LexisNexis.

line." This feature displays the over 400 topics of the *American Digest System* as if the researcher were browsing the digest shelves. Clicking the "+" symbol next to a topic will reveal subtopics and key numbers. When a promising topic and key number are located, a search can be performed to locate relevant cases from the appropriate jurisdiction. Figure 11-5 illustrates this feature.

Digest and citator features on both Westlaw and LexisNexis can also be utilized when you have "one good case" to begin your research.

Figure 11-5. West Key Number Digest Outline

Source: Westlaw. Reprinted with permission of Thomson Reuters/West.

Suppose you find a helpful case. In LexisNexis, you can immediately Shepardize the case to learn of subsequent cases and secondary authorities that cited it. By restricting the Shepard's search to relevant headnotes, you can narrow your search to those subsequent cases that are most likely to be helpful in your research. Alternatively, clicking on a headnote will lead to a screen that allows searching for other cases LexisNexis has indexed under the same topic. Other LexisNexis options include the "More Like This" or "More Like Selected Text" functions, which ask the computer to find other cases with similar citations or similar language.

Figure 11-6. Westlaw's KeySearch

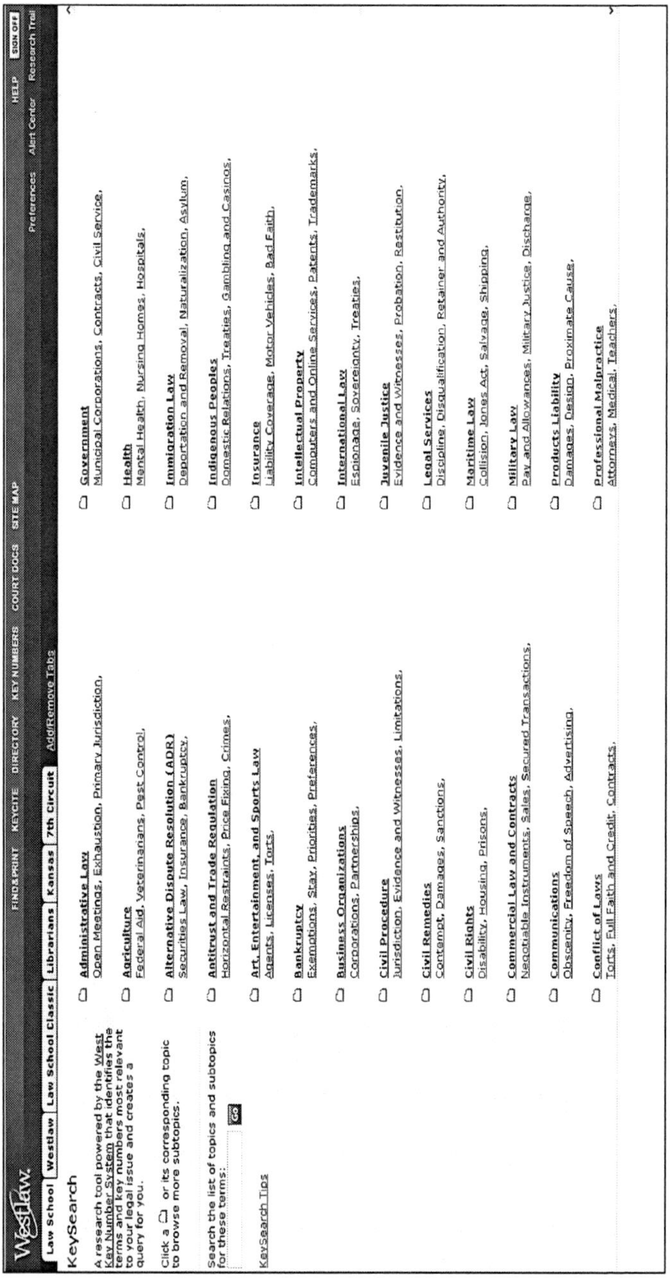

Source: Westlaw. Reprinted with permission of Thomson Reuters/West.

The Westlaw equivalent to Shepardizing is to use the "KeyCite" function, which will list cases and other authorities that cited your case, and allow you to restrict the results similarly to Shepard's on LexisNexis. Furthermore, the *American Digest System* can be used quite effectively when you begin with "one good case." Review a case on point to identify the topic-key numbers for relevant headnotes. Clicking on the key number in a case will bring up a screen that prompts a search for additional cases with that key number. This process is very similar to the print digest research discussed extensively in Chapter 5. Indeed, those familiar with print digests will find this feature to be fairly intuitive.

Computer-assisted legal research has also given rise to new variations on the theme of digest research that merge the best aspects of print and electronic resources. "KeySearch," found on Westlaw, and "Search by Topic or Headnote" on LexisNexis represent the newest generation of online resources that combine the structure of digest systems with the power of electronic databases. As noted in Chapter 1, these tools allow the researcher to begin with a list of broad areas of law and narrow the topic by clicking through successive lists. As with the more traditional ways of accessing digests, when a promising digest topic is located, a search can be performed to locate relevant cases from the appropriate jurisdiction. Figure 11-6 illustrates the Westlaw "KeySearch" feature, while Figure 11-7 depicts the Lexis-Nexis "Search by Topic or Headnote" screen.

D. Printing, Downloading, or Emailing Results

Both LexisNexis and Westlaw allow you to download or email documents as opposed to printing them. Now that most word processors allow highlighting and in-line annotating, you may choose to read and organize your research documents entirely on your computer. Remember, however, that you must read (and often re-read) relevant documents very carefully, and many researchers still find it easier to do so on paper as opposed to the computer screen.

Figure 11-7. Search by Topic or Headnote on LexisNexis

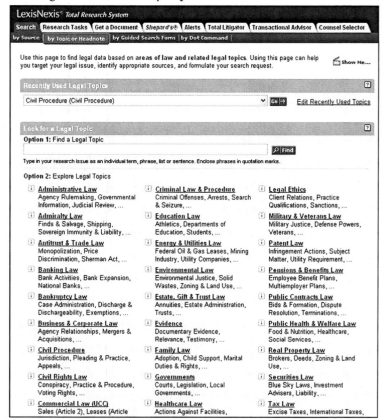

Source: LexisNexis. Copyright 2008 LexisNexis, a division of Reed Elsevier Inc. All Rights Reserved. LexisNexis and the Knowledge Burst logo are registered trademarks of Reed Elsevier Properties Inc. and are used with the permission of LexisNexis.

E. Keeping Track

If you are new to online legal searches, your searches may be more successful if you complete the chart in Table 11-8 before beginning your search. Even after you become experienced in online searching, you should still keep notes containing the dates you searched, the searches you ran, and your results from the searches.

Table 11-8. Example Notes for Online Searching

Date of Search:	*January 1, 2008*
Issue:	*After a mistrial, can a defendant in Kansas file an interlocutory appeal on double jeopardy grounds?*
Online Site or Service:	*Westlaw*
Sources:	*Kansas State Courts (short name: KS-CS)*
Search Terms:	*mistrial, interlocutory appeal, double jeopardy*
Date Restriction:	*None*
Search:	*mistrial & interlocutory /p "double jeopardy"*
Results:	*[Either list your results here or print a cite list to attach to your notes.]*

These notes will help you stay on track and avoid duplicating research on a later date. Notes will also indicate the time period that needs to be updated as you near your project deadline. In addition, online services provide lists of past searches and results, and you should form the habit of printing or saving them. On LexisNexis, click "History." On Westlaw, click "Research Trail." However, be aware that these features typically expire within two to four weeks.

Appendix
Where to Find Kansas Law

Below is a list of sources for Kansas law in print, on state government websites, and on LexisNexis and Westlaw. The list is not exhaustive, especially with regard to online databases. (Note that the abbreviations for Westlaw databases and LexisNexis sources are available on the scope page, indicated by an "i" next to the database or source name.)

Kansas Constitution

Print sources	*Kansas Statutes Annotated*
Government website	www.kslib.info/constitution/index.html
LexisNexis	KSCNST
Westlaw	KS-ST or KS-ST-ANN

Statutes

Print sources	*Kansas Statutes Annotated*
Government website	www.kslegislature.org/legsrv-statutes/index.do
LexisNexis	KSCODE
Westlaw	KS-ST or KS-ST-ANN

Legislative History

Print sources	*Session Laws of Kansas*
	Kansas Senate and House Bills
	Kansas Legislative Interim Studies
	Committee Minutes
	Journal of the House
	Journal of the Senate
Government websites	www.kslegislature.org
	http://skyways.lib.ks.us/ksleg/KLRD/klrd.html
LexisNexis	KSLH
Westlaw	KS-LH

Agency Rules

Print sources	*Kansas Administrative Regulations*
	Kansas Register
Government websites	www.kslegislature.org/legsrv-kars/index.do
	www.kssos.org/pubs/pubs_kansas_register.asp
LexisNexis	KSREGS
Westlaw	KS-ADC

Judicial Opinions

Print sources	*Kansas Digest 2d*
	Kansas Reports
	Kansas Court of Appeals Reports, Second
	Pacific Digest
	Pacific Reporter
Government website	www.kscourts.org
LexisNexis	KSCTS
Westlaw	KS-CS

Court Rules

Print sources	*West's Kansas Court Rules and Procedure (State)*
	West's Kansas Court Rules for Judicial Districts (Local)
Government website	www.kscourts.org
LexisNexis	KSRULE
Westlaw	KS-RULES

Updating

Print sources	*Shepard's Kansas Citations*
	Shepard's Pacific Reporter Citations
LexisNexis	Shepard's
Westlaw	KeyCite

Chapter 12

Research Strategies and Organization

I. Moving from Story to Strategy

The purpose of legal research is to solve a client's problem. Each client presents his problem to a lawyer in the form of a story; in telling his story, the client focuses on facts that are important to him, without regard to whether they are legally significant. The lawyer may need to ask questions to probe for facts the client may not immediately remember but which may have important legal consequences. The lawyer may also need to review documents such as contracts, letters, bills, or public records. It may also be necessary to interview other people who are involved in the client's situation.

In sifting through the client's story, the lawyer determines which legal issues are involved. Sometimes a lawyer cannot immediately identify the legal issues involved in a particular situation. Especially in an unfamiliar area of law, the lawyer may need to do some initial research to learn about the legal issues that affect the client's situation.

After understanding the facts and identifying the legal issues, the lawyer conducts research to determine what the law is and how to solve the client's problem.[1] This chapter explains how to develop a strategy for conducting research efficiently and offers suggestions for organizing the documents pertinent to the problem.

---

1. Sometimes the solution desired by the client may be better obtained through mediation, family counseling, management strategies, or other means.

II. Planning Your Research Strategy

The research process presented in Chapter 1 contains seven steps: (1) generate a list of *research terms*; (2) consult *secondary sources*; (3) find controlling *constitutional provisions, statutes,* or *administrative rules*; (4) use *digests* or *online databases* to find citations to cases; (5) *read* the cases; (6) *update* your legal authorities with a citator; and (7) *end* your research when you have no holes in your analysis and when you begin seeing the same authorities repeatedly.

This basic process can be modified for a specific project. When researching an unfamiliar area of law, you will probably be more successful beginning with secondary sources. In contrast, if you are familiar with an area of statutory law from previous work, your research may be more effective if you go directly to an annotated code. As a third example, if you are working for another attorney who gives you a citation to a case she knows is relevant, you may want to begin by Shepardizing or KeyCiting the case, or using its topic-key numbers in a West digest. Both steps may quickly provide more cases on point. Finally, if your supervisor knows the issue is controlled by common law, you may feel comfortable not researching statutory or constitutional provisions, or spending very little time in those areas.

The research process is not necessarily linear. Research terms are useful in searching the indexes of secondary sources and statutes as well as digests. Secondary sources may cite relevant statutes or cases. Updating may reveal more cases that you need to read, or it may uncover a new law review article that is on point. As you learn more about a project, you may want to review whether your earlier research was effective. Even as you begin writing, you may need to do more research if new issues arise or if you need more support for an argument. The flow chart in Table 12-1 gives an idea of how this process works.[2]

---

2. To simplify an already complicated flow chart, constitutional provisions, administrative law, and legislative history are omitted.

Table 12-1. The Recursive Process of Research

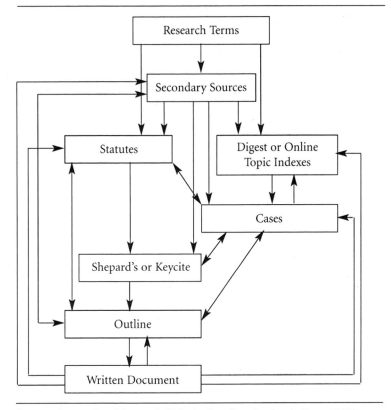

Source: *Oregon Legal Research* (2d ed., Carolina Academic Press 2007).

III. Organizing Research

Keeping research organized is a means to efficient research, not an end in itself. The only "right" way to organize your research is the way that best helps you perform effective research, understand the legal issues, and analyze the problem. The following method will work for taking notes either on a laptop or on a legal pad. For researchers working with paper and pen, "create a document" simply means turning to a new page in a legal pad. Consider using color-coded sticky notes to tab each new document so that you do not get lost in a sea of paper. Some researchers prefer to keep notes of primary authorities on index cards rather than on sheets of paper or in computer files. If so, you will need some sort of box or a combination of clips and rubber bands to keep the cards organized.

Take careful notes throughout the research process. Taking notes can help you avoid duplicating steps, especially if you have to interrupt your research for a notable length of time. Analytical notes also provide a basis for organizing and writing your document. These notes do not have to be formal or typed; in fact, you might waste valuable time by following too much structure or stopping to type notes.

Do not underestimate the learning process that occurs while taking notes. Deciding what is important enough to include in notes and expressing those ideas in your own words will increase your understanding of the legal issues involved. Pressing the "print" key and highlighting do not provide this same analytical advantage.

Regardless of whether you take notes on your computer or on paper, you will need a three-ring binder or a set of files in which you keep hard copies of the most important authorities. Tab the binder or label the files with the following headings: strategy/process; secondary sources; list of primary authorities; statutes (include rules and constitutional provisions here); cases; updating; and outline.

Keep organization in perspective. Spending extra time tabbing documents may make you more efficient, or it may be a form of procrastination.

A. Strategy and Process Trail

The first document you create should be your research *strategy*. This is simply a list of the different types of legal resources you intend to search. Writing out a strategy will help you ensure that you check all relevant sources of law. It may also make a new project seem less overwhelming, since the strategy will contain definite steps. You should refer to this document frequently to be sure you are keeping on track. In developing your strategy, remember to ask the following questions:

- Is this issue controlled by state law, federal law, or both?
- Are there statutes or constitutional provisions on point or is this an area left to common law?
- Are administrative rules or decisions likely to be involved?
- Where in the research process will online sources be more effective and cost efficient than print sources?
- What period of time needs to be researched?
- How long do I have to complete the project?

Feel free to revise your strategy as you learn more about the issues. For instance, you may read a case with a related cause of action that you had not considered or you may encounter an article that highlights a relevant federal claim. If so, you need to adjust your research accordingly.

Your strategy should include a list of research terms that you generate from the facts and issues of your research problem. Brainstorm broadly to develop an expansive list. Refer to this list as you begin work in each new resource. Note on the list which terms were helpful in which resource. Add new terms to the list as you discover them. This list is especially likely to grow during your initial efforts if you begin with a secondary source that provides context for the research project.

Next, begin a *process trail*. While the strategy document outlines what you intend to do in your research, the process trail records what you actually did. By comparing the two, you will stay on track in your research and avoid duplicating work. Some researchers keep copious notes on their strategy document, so that in essence it becomes the process trail. With experience, you will develop a system that is comfortable and efficient for you.

As you begin with a new resource, make notes in your process trail that summarize your work in that resource. For print research, include the volumes you used, the indexes or tables you reviewed, and the terms you searched for. For computer research, include the site, the specific database or link, and the searches that you entered. List both successful and unsuccessful index terms and searches so that you do not inadvertently repeat these same steps later, or so you can revisit a "dead end" that later becomes relevant. Note the date that you performed each search.

B. Secondary Authorities

It is good practice, after consulting a particular secondary source, to write out a paragraph summary on how you analyzed and applied the information to your particular fact situation. Begin to organize your analysis of the problem. By doing this when perusing secondary authority, you will save research time by identifying those issues which need more research and what the next logical research source will be. After writing these summaries, you should be able to identify the issues, have relevant statute and case law references, and have a good sense of where you need to go next. For example, after consulting an initial secondary source, you might want to make sure a particular statute referenced by a law review article has not been amended, or you might want to use a citator on the interesting case you found mentioned in a footnote from a leading treatise.

C. List of Primary Authorities

From your initial work with the secondary authority summaries, create a list that contains the name and citation for all the primary authorities you need to read. Throughout your research, as you come across a potentially relevant authority, include it on the list. This method will allow you to maintain your train of thought with one resource while ensuring that you keep track of important cites to check later. After creating a list that includes a number of sources, check for duplicates before reading the authorities.

D. Analytical Notes of Primary Authorities

Legal analysis must be based on your reading of the relevant statutes and cases:

Read the statutes and the cases! No digest, treatise, or case synopsis service can be a foolproof legal research tool. More often than not, the resources described in a digest, book, or article only provide the analytical framework for a substantive or procedural issue. Without a complete review of the cases, and thorough updating for more recent cases and statutes, a lawyer may find in the courtroom that incomplete research will snatch defeat from the jaws of victory.[3]

Reading legal authorities is one of the most time-consuming activities for a novice researcher, but the following suggestions may help. For statutes and rules, skim through sections that provide definitions or explain the purpose. Focus on operative language that sets out duties or proscribes certain conduct. Quickly glance at provisions codified just before or after your provisions to see whether they are relevant. For cases, begin by reading the synopsis at the beginning of the case. Then skim the headnotes to find the portion of the case that is possibly on point. Go directly to that portion of the case and read it. This probably means skipping over the procedural history, the facts of the case, and analysis of unrelated points of law.

If the source contains relevant material, make a few notes on your list of authorities. If it is not relevant, strike through it on the list. If you are on a computer, use the "reviewing" or "commenting" toolbar to strike through these authorities. Do not completely delete or erase irrelevant authorities; otherwise, you may later find yourself accidentally reading them again.

Once you have selected a number of relevant authorities, choose an organizational scheme for reading them carefully in groups. If there is a constitutional provision, statute, or rule on point, begin by reading it carefully, then move to reading cases that interpret the provision. One approach is to read cases in chronological order, so that you see the development of the law over time. This approach may be time consuming for causes of action that have existed for many years.

---

3. William Goodman, *Essential Research Tools for Criminal Defense Attorneys*, 1 Legal Ref. Servs. Q. 5 (1981).

Except for historical research, impose an artificial cut-off of twenty or thirty years in the past, so that you put your effort in recent law. The opposite approach works in many situations: by beginning with the recent cases, you avoid spending time learning old law that has been revised or superseded.

After organizing relevant authorities, read them carefully. In this second, slower reading, pay attention to parts that you may have skipped earlier while skimming. Read carefully the definitions in statutes. Be sure you understand the procedural posture of each case, since this affects the standard of review applied. Also be sure that you understand the facts of cases. Drawing a time line or a chart of the relationships between the parties may be helpful. As you read through the case, cross out portions dealing with legal issues that are not confronting your client. If you decide that the case is actually not important, mark that on the first page so that you will not waste time reading it again.

When researching several issues or related claims, consider them one at a time. In this instance you may have several lists of primary authorities, one for each claim you are researching. You may want to create a different binder or set of folders for each claim.

1. Notes on Statutes

Notes on relevant statutes should include both the actual statutory language and your outline of it. Because the exact words of statutes are so important, you should print, photocopy, or electronically save the text of these provisions. To fully understand a complex statute, you should outline it. Highlighting is sufficient only if the statute is very short and clear. The statute may provide the elements of the claim or may control the period in which a claim can be brought. Outlining each statute will help you understand it better.

Be sure to refer to the definition sections of statutes; where important terms are not defined, make a note to look for judicial definitions. Also be sure to read statutes that are cross-referenced in any pertinent statute.

2. Notes on Cases

If a case is relevant, brief it. The brief does not have to follow any formal style. Instead, the brief for each case should be a set of notes that highlight the key aspects of the case that are relevant for your research problem. Create a short summary of the pertinent facts, holding, and reasoning. You may choose to do this on your computer, creating a document or a page of a document for each case. You might prefer to write your summary in your legal pad or create an index card. Each case brief should include the following:

- *Citation.* Including the full citation will make writing the document easier because you avoid referring back to the original.
- *Facts.* Include only those facts that are relevant to your project.
- *Holding and reasoning.* Summarize the court's analysis. Again, address only those issues in the case that are relevant to your project. For example, if a case includes both a tort claim and a related contract claim, but the contract claim is not relevant to your project, there is no need for you to thoroughly understand and take notes on the contract claim. Skim that section to be sure there is no relevant information hidden there, then ignore it.
- *Pinpoint pages.* For case information that you will cite in a written document, include the pinpoint cite. Be sure that the pinpoint is to the reporter you have been asked to cite in your document, not a parallel cite. Attention to detail is especially important when printing online documents in which pagination in different reporters is indicated solely by an asterisk or two.
- *Reflections.* Include your thoughts on the case: How do you anticipate using this case in your analysis? Does it resolve certain issues for your problem? Does it raise new questions?
- *Updating information.* Each case briefed should have a designated space for updating. Whether you use Shepard's or KeyCite, you must update each case that you use in your analysis.

E. Updating

You will likely find yourself updating at several points during the research process. Updating with Shepard's or KeyCite early in the process will lead to other authorities on point. Updating before you begin to rely on an authority is critical; you must verify that each authority you include in your analysis is still "good law." Updating just before submitting a document ensures that nothing has changed while you were working on the project. Recording the date of your initial updating search will be helpful when you perform your final update just before submitting your document because you will only have to check citing sources that became available in the interim.

Printing lists of citations is an easy and efficient way to compare new citations with your list of primary authorities. Keep these citation lists in the *updating* section of your binder.

F. Outlining the Analysis

Because the most effective research often occurs in conjunction with the analysis of a particular project, try to develop an outline that addresses your client's problem as soon as you can. If outlining feels too restrictive, you may benefit from a chart that organizes all the primary authority by issue or element, such as in Table 12-2.

Your first analytical outline or chart may be based on information in a secondary source, the requirements of a statute, or the elements of a common law claim. It will become more sophisticated and detailed as you conduct your research. Recognize that you cannot reread every case or statute in its entirety each time you need to include it in your outline; instead, refer to your notes and briefs to find the key ideas supporting each step in your analysis.

The outline or chart should enable you to synthesize the law, apply the law to your client's facts, and reach a conclusion on the desired outcome. Applying the law to your client's facts may lead you to research issues that may not be apparent in a merely theoretical discussion of law.

Table 12-2. Sample Analysis Chart

Research Question: Has a person committed burglary in the State of Kansas if she entered a house that had partially burned in a fire for the purpose of selling a large quantity of drugs?

Controlling Statute: K.S.A. 21-3715 (2007), "Burglary is knowingly and without authority entering into or remaining within any:

(a) Building, manufactured home, mobile home, tent or other structure *which is a dwelling*, with intent to commit a felony, theft or sexual battery therein;

(b) building, manufactured home, mobile home, tent or other structure *which is not a dwelling*, with intent to commit a felony, theft or sexual battery therein.

Case	General Rule	Facts of the Case	Holding
Herrick v. State, 965 P.2d 844	Definition of dwelling used in the Kansas statutes is particularly broad. A dwelling is not only a building which is used as a human habitation, home, or residence, but one that is intended for use as one.	The building in this case with screen doors, windows and pieces of wood lying all over the house and currently not lived in did not have to be presently used as human habitation, home or residence for it to be considered a dwelling.	Building in question was intended for use as a home, although it was not being used that way at the time of the burglary.
State v. Alvis, 53 P.3d 1232	To classify a house under construction as a "dwelling" for purposes of the burglary statute, it must be shown that the house was capable of human habitation.	House was under construction, had not yet been lived in, and might be incapable of human habitation.	The record was so lacking in information regarding the house's condition that court cannot conclude the house qualified as a dwelling. The State simply did not carry its burden in this regard. Court noted the purpose for making a burglary involving a dwelling a felony is to prevent contact with people. Court believed holding in this case comports with this objective and the reasoning set forth in *Herrick.*

Table 12-2. Sample Analysis Chart, *continued*

State v. Story, 154 P.3d 1148	A reading of the burglary statute does not require that a building that is not a dwelling be completely enclosed or that it present a barrier to entry before it constitutes a building under the statute.	A structure that will become a hospital, and which is 70% complete with four walls, a roof, and a floor is a building under the Kansas burglary statute.	Under a plain reading of the Kansas statute combined with the weight of authority from other states, court concluded that the unfinished building that defendant entered and from which he stole a saw constituted a building as mentioned in KSA 21-3715(b).

G. Ending Research

One of the most difficult problems new researchers face is deciding when to stop researching and begin writing. Often deadlines imposed by the court or a supervisor will limit the amount of time spent on a research project. The expense to the client will also be a consideration.

Apart from these practical constraints, most legal researchers want to believe if they search long enough they will find a case or statute or article or *something* that answers the client's legal question clearly and definitively. Sometimes that happens; if you find the answer, you know your research is over. Even without finding a clear answer, when your research in various sources leads back to the same authorities, you can be confident that you have been thorough. As a final checklist, go through each step of the basic research process to ensure you considered each one. Then review your strategy and process trail for this particular project.

If you have worked through the research process and found nothing, it may be that nothing exists. Before reaching that conclusion, expand your research terms and look in a few more secondary sources. Consider whether other jurisdictions may have helpful persuasive authority.

Remember that the goal of legal research is to solve a client's problem. Sometimes the law will not seem to support the solution that your client had in mind. Think creatively to address the client's problem in a different way. While you must tell your supervisor or your client when a desired approach is not feasible, you will want to have prepared an alternate solution if possible.

Appendix A

Legal Citation

Legal arguments often synthesize several different authorities found in several different publications. Accordingly, legal writing requires precise citation to these authorities and publications. In a legal document, every legal rule and every exposition of the law must be supported with specific citations to authority. These legal citations tell the reader where to find the authorities relied on and indicate the level of analytical support the authorities provide.[1] (See Table A-1.)

This requirement, mundane and arcane to the uninitiated, plays a significant role in the legal profession. In fact, painstaking attention to detail is the hallmark of the professional culture surrounding legal citation. This tradition ensures effective communication between all parties and brings order to the vast frontier of competing authorities. A legal document must convince a lawyer or judge reading it that its arguments were well researched and its conclusions well supported. Sloppy citations reflect poorly upon even the most brilliant analysis. The practical reality is that flawless legal citation is a threshold for credibility and is a prerequisite for all legal writing.

Legal citation involves far more than a simple bibliography. Practitioners usually provide citations for all relevant authority within the main text of the document. Similarly, academic legal works typically include innumerable footnotes for each significant proposition of law and fact. While law students often initially feel that these citations clutter documents, they soon learn to appreciate the valuable research leads that citations provide.

---

1. Association of Legal Writing Directors & Darby Dickerson, *ALWD Citation Manual* 3 (3d ed., Aspen Publishers 2006) ("*ALWD Manual*").

Table A-1. Purposes of Legal Citations

- Show the reader where to find the cited material in the original case, state, rule, article, or other authority.
- Indicate the weight and persuasiveness of each authority, for example, by specifying the court that decided the case, the author of a document, and the publication date of the authority.
- Convey the type and degree of support the authority offers, for example, by indicating whether the authority supports your point directly or only implicitly.
- Demonstrate that the analysis in your document is the result of careful research.

Source: ALWD Manual.

The format used to convey citation information requires meticulous attention to such details as whether a space is needed between two abbreviations. In this respect, citation format rules are like fundamental writing rules, which are based on convention, not reason. Rather than trying to understand why citations are formatted the way they are, the most practical approach is simply to learn citation rules and apply them.

While frequent repetition can make legal citation second nature, the process is not always intuitive because there is not one consensus method of citation. Rather, there are two national citation manuals, the *ALWD Citation Manual: A Professional System of Citation*[2] and *The Bluebook: A Uniform System of Citation.*[3] There is also a less widely used manual entitled the *Maroonbook.*[4]

---

2. *Id.*

3. *The Bluebook: A Uniform System of Citation* (The Columbia Law Review et al. eds., 18th ed., The Harvard Law Review Assn. 2005) ("*Bluebook*").

4. Promulgated by the University of Chicago, the *Maroonbook* can be found at http://lawreview.uchicago.edu/resources/style_sheet.html.

Further complicating matters, countless variations on these themes can be found in different legal environments throughout the country. In law practice, you may encounter state statutes, court rules, and style manuals that dictate the form of citation used before the courts of different states. You may find that each firm or agency that you work for has its own preference for citation or makes minor variations to generally accepted format. Some law offices have their own style manuals, drawn from state rules and national manuals.

Thus, citation practices will always be a function of the audience you are writing for. However, there is a silver lining: most variations, even between the two national citation manuals, are minor. Indeed, there are general patterns that all legal citation styles follow, with the differences being found only in the details. Once you are aware of the basic function and format of citation, adapting to a slightly different set of rules is not difficult.

I. The *Bluebook*

Student editors of four Ivy League law reviews have developed citation rules that are published as *The Bluebook: A Uniform System of Citation*, soon to be in its nineteenth edition. Until the *ALWD Manual* was first published in 2000, the *Bluebook* was the only national citation system that was widely recognized. Indeed, the term "Bluebooking" has become synonymous with checking legal citations for accuracy.

The *Bluebook* actually includes *two* citation systems: one for law review articles and another for legal memoranda and court documents. Learning to navigate this bifurcated scheme of voluminous rules, tables, and cross-references has long been a rite of passage for law students. Most quickly learn to consult the "Quick Reference" tables early and often. The Quick Reference table found in the front of the *Bluebook* provides citation templates for law review footnotes. The Quick Reference table found in the back of the *Bluebook* does the same for court documents and legal memoranda. Use of these features facilitates efficient citation. However, it is usually necessary to consult the corresponding rules and tables within the *Bluebook* to ensure no minutia is overlooked.

II. The *ALWD Manual*

The byzantine qualities of the *Bluebook* have stimulated efforts to simplify the process of legal citation. The *ALWD Manual* was created by the Association of Legal Writing Directors "because lawyers, judges, law teachers, and law students need a citation manual that is easy to use, easy to teach from, and easy to learn from."[5] The *ALWD Manual* has managed to challenge the hegemony of the *Bluebook*; however, "since it aims to reflect current usage, it is highly consistent with *The Bluebook*."[6] Most of the differences between the two are minor, and usually stem from the *ALWD Manual*'s use of a single system of citation for legal memoranda, court documents, law review articles, and all other legal documents.

III. Legal Citation in Kansas

Some states offer comprehensive documents governing legal citation. California and New York, for example, each publish a style manual that speaks specifically to citing conventions. In contrast, legal citations in Kansas are not extensively codified and are largely based upon tradition and the *Bluebook*. However, to reiterate, there can be significant variation within this regime. A local trial court may have citation preferences that differ from state appellate practice prescriptions, while federal courts can be a different animal altogether. Likewise, citations in a Kansas law firm's internal memoranda will not look the same as citations in an article submitted to a Kansas law review or journal. Again, knowing the audience you are writing for is crucial.

---

5. *ALWD Manual* Preface, xxiii.
6. Peter W. Martin, *Introduction to Basic Legal Citation* (LII 2007 ed.), www.law.cornell.edu/citation.

Table A-2. Citing Kansas Statutes

Bluebook	KAN. STAT. ANN. §60-1501 (Year)
ALWD Manual	Kan. Stat. Ann. §60-1501 (Year)
Kansas	K.S.A. 60-1501 (Year)

Contrasting the *Bluebook*,[7] the *ALWD Manual*, and Kansas's customary citing conventions illustrates the nuanced character of legal citation. Table A-2 compares the three approaches to citing codified Kansas statutes. The more heavily abbreviated Kansas approach, dictated on the title pages of *Kansas Statutes Annotated* volumes, reflects the difference between writing for national and local audiences.

Regarding the citation of Kansas cases, it is important to consult Kansas Supreme Court Rule 6.08. This rule advises that, in appellate briefs, "[r]eferences to court cases shall be by the official citations followed by any generally recognized reporter system citations." The practice of providing citations to both official reporters and commercial regional reporters is known as *parallel citation*. Table A-3 depicts how a Kansas case can be cited in this manner. Note that, despite differences in the treatment of case names, all three approaches follow the *volume-publication-page* format. This pattern holds true throughout most citations to reporters and other chronological publications.

Additional information must be provided when quoting or providing specific information from a source. The specific page where the passage can be located must be inserted into the citation. This practice is known as *pinpoint citation*, and it is more complicated when providing parallel citations to multiple reporters. Using the case in Table A-3 as an example, the same sentence appears on page 526 of the official *Kansas Reports* and on page 244 of the *Pacific Reporter*. To cite that sentence, these page numbers are included after the page number indicating the beginning of the case: *Rose v. Via Christi Health System, Inc.*, 279 Kan. 523, 526, 113 P.3d 241, 244 (2005).

---

7. Remember that the *Bluebook* has two sets of conventions, one for law review footnotes and another for court documents and legal memoranda. The example shown in Table A-2 is for law review footnotes. The style for practice documents is exactly the same as the *ALWD* example.

Table A-3. Citing Kansas Cases

Bluebook* (Court Documents & Legal Memoranda)	<u>Rose v. Via Christi Health System, Inc.</u>, 279 Kan. 523, 113 P.3d 241 (2005)
Bluebook (Law Review Footnotes)	Rose v. Via Christi Health System, Inc., 279 Kan. 523, 113 P.3d 241 (2005)
ALWD Manual*	*Rose v. Via Christi Health System, Inc.*, 279 Kan. 523, 113 P.3d 241 (2005)

* In the *Bluebook* and the *ALWD Manual*, underlining and italics are identical. The key is to select one format and use it consistently throughout a document.

IV. Conclusion

This short discussion is intended only to provide a glimpse into the complex world of legal citation. Citing publications other than statutes and cases, using introductory signals, mastering short-citation forms and abbreviations, adapting to the new wave of public domain formats—all of these skills and many more must be internalized by members of the legal profession. It is impracticable to include a detailed examination of every facet of legal citation here. Regardless, merely reading about the rules of legal citation would not be a very effective way to master the information. Rather, learning legal citation is an interactive process that requires hours of hands-on experience.

Appendix B

Selected List of Kansas Practice Materials

The titles included here are standard practice books. Books that have not been updated within the past ten years are not included. Additional titles and updates are available from each publisher's website.

Subject Headings:

Administrative Law

Alternative Dispute Resolution

Bankruptcy Law

Business/Corporate/Commercial Law

Civil Procedure

Collections

Construction Law

Criminal Law

Elder Law

Employment and Labor Law

Estate Planning

Ethics

Evidence

Family Law

Insurance Law

Jury Instructions

Legal Research

Local Government Law

Oil and Gas Law

Practice of Law

Real Estate Practice Law

School Law

Sentencing Guidelines

Tax Law

Trial/Appellate Practice

Workers' Compensation

Administrative Law

Kansas Administrative Law from the Viewpoint of Decision Makers (Kansas Bar Assn. 2002).

Alternative Dispute Resolution

Alternative Dispute Resolution (Kansas Bar Assn. 2001).

Bankruptcy Law

Kansas Bankruptcy Law (Kansas Bar Assn. 2001).

Jonathan C. Becker, *Life After Bankruptcy Reform? – One Year Later* (Natl. Bus. Inst. 2006).

Kathryn B. Bussing et al., *Fundamentals of Bankruptcy Law and Procedure in Kansas* (Natl. Bus. Inst. 1999).

Michael D. Doering et al., *Bankruptcy Law and Procedure From Start to Finish* (Natl. Bus. Inst. 2007).

Business/Corporate/Commercial Law

Denise M. Anderson et al., *Legal and Practical Considerations for Operating a Small Business in Kansas* (Natl. Bus. Inst. 2006).

Edwin W. Hecker, Jr. et al., *Limited Liability Companies* (Kansas Bar Assn. 2002).

Michael L. McCann et al., *Limited Liability Companies in Kansas* (Natl. Bus. Inst. 2004).

Civil Procedure

Spencer A. Gard & Robert C. Casad, *Kansas Code of Civil Procedure Annotated* (4th ed., West 2003 with 2007 Supp.). Available on Westlaw.

Collections

David J. Berkowitz et al., *Collecting Debts: Tips and Strategies to Legally Get What You're Owed* (Natl. Bus. Inst. 2006).

Construction Law

Construction Law (Kansas Bar Assn. 1999).

Harold A. Houck & Kevin J. Breer, *Kansas Construction Law Handbook* (Kansas Bar Assn. 2006). (KBA Practice Handbook). Available on LexisNexis.

Christopher J. Mohart et al., *Resolving Problems and Disputes on Construction Projects* (Natl. Bus. Inst. 2007).

Criminal Law

Elizabeth Cateforis, *Kansas Criminal Law Handbook* (4th ed., Kansas Bar Assn. 2006). (KBA Practice Handbook). Available on Lexis-Nexis.

Elder Law

James P. Berger et al., *Elder Care in Kansas: Legal and Financial Issues* (Natl. Bus. Inst. 2004).

Molly M. Wood et al., *2006 Elder Law Institute: Growing Concerns for a Graying Community* (Kansas Bar Assn. 2006).

Molly M. Wood, *Kansas Long-Term Care Handbook* (Kansas Bar Assn. 1999 with 2001 Supp.). (KBA Practice Handbook). Available on LexisNexis.

Molly M. Wood et al., *Legal Assistance for Frail, Elderly Kansans* (Natl. Bus. Inst. 2005).

Employment and Labor Law

Employment Law: Employment Litigation (Kansas Bar Assn. 2000).

Michael F. Brady et al., *Wage and Hour Claims: A Practical Guide to Claim Resolution* (Natl. Bus. Inst. 2007).

Joseph R. Colantuono et al., *Basic Wage and Hour Law in Kansas* (Natl. Bus. Inst. 1999).

Glenn S. Grayson et al., *Kansas Labor and Employment Law* (Natl. Bus. Inst. 1999).

Kip A. Kubin et al., *Kansas Labor and Employment Law* (Natl. Bus. Inst. 2004).

Elinor P. Schroeder, *Kansas Employment Law* (2d ed., Kansas Bar Assn. 2001). (KBA Practice Handbook). Available on LexisNexis.

Estate Planning

Kansas Estate Administration Handbook (6th ed., Kansas Bar Assn. 1993 with 1997 and 1999 Supps.). Available on LexisNexis.

Robert A. Andrews et al., *Estate Administration Procedures: Why Each Step Is Important* (Natl. Bus. Inst. 2006).

Kelly Dean Brende et al., *Probate Practice: The Essential Basics* (Natl. Bus. Inst. 2007).

Donald D. Friend II et al., *Estate Planning Basics* (Natl. Bus. Inst. 2007).

Hellen Hague & Robert Hughes, *Basic Will Drafting: With Discussion of Revocable Trusts* (Kansas Bar Assn. 2001).

B.J. Hickert et al., *Basic Probate Procedures and Practice in Kansas* (Natl. Bus. Inst. 1999).

Kansas Judicial Council, *Kansas Judicial Council Probate Forms* (2d ed., Kansas Bar Assn. 2004 with 2007 Supp.).

Ethics

Mark F. Anderson et al., *Kansas Ethics Handbook* (Kansas Bar Assn. 1996 with 2001 Supp.). (KBA Practice Handbook). Available on LexisNexis.

William F. Logan et al., *Managing Ethical Issues in Your Day-to-Day Practice* (Natl. Bus. Inst. 2007).

Evidence

Michael A. Barbara, *Lawyers Guide to Kansas Evidence* (5th ed., West 2007).

Family Law

Richard D. Dvorak et al., *Family Law in Kansas* (Natl. Bus. Inst. 1999).

James Buchele, *Kansas Family Law* (West 1999 with 2007 Supp.).

Honorable Allen Slater et al., *What Family Court Judges Want You to Know* (Natl. Bus. Inst. 2007).

Kansas Family Law Institute (Kansas Bar Assn. 2001).

Honorable Steve Leben et al., *Practitioner's Guide to Kansas Family Law* (Kansas Bar Assn. 1997 with 2004 Supp.). (KBA Practice Handbook). Available on LexisNexis.

Insurance Law

Craig C. Blumreich et al., *Insurance Coverage Law in Kansas* (Natl. Bus. Inst. 1999).

Randall E. Fisher, *Kansas Automotive Insurance Law* (Kansas Auto Insurance Lawbook 2006).

Patrick E. McGrath et al., *Vexatious Refusal & Bad Faith Insurance in Kansas* (Natl. Bus. Inst. 2007).

Kathleen A. Ryan et al., *Insurance Coverage Litigation* (Natl. Bus. Inst. 2007).

Jury Instructions

Kansas Judicial Council, *Pattern Instruction Kansas* (3d ed., West 1997 with 2005 Supp.)

Kansas Judicial Council Advisory Committee on Criminal Jury Instructions, *Pattern Instruction for Kansas – Criminal* (3d ed., Kansas Judicial Council 1993 with 2006 Supp.).

Legal Research

Joseph A. Custer, *Kansas Legal Research and Reference Guide* (3d ed., Kansas Bar Assn. 2003). (KBA Practice Handbook).

Christopher Steadham et al., *Find It Free and Fast on the Net: Strategies for Legal Research on the Web* (Natl. Bus. Inst. 2007).

Local Government Law

Michael R. Heim, *Kansas Local Government Law* (3d ed., League of Kansas Municipalities 2005).

Oil and Gas Law

KBA/KIOGA Oil & Gas Conference (Kansas Bar Assn. 2003).

Practice of Law

Kansas Solo and Small Firm Conference (Kansas Bar Assn. 2001).

Practical Skills for New Lawyers (Kansas Bar Assn. 2004).

Joseph Custer et al., *Survival Kansas: The Solo and Small Firm Edition* (Kansas Bar Assn. 2007).

Real Estate Practice Law

Kansas Title Standards Handbook (7th ed., Kansas Bar Assn. 2005). Available on LexisNexis.

Thomas E. Beall et al., *Real Estate Litigation in Kansas* (Natl. Bus. Inst. 2007).

Carl J. Circo & Louis A. Heaven, Jr., *Kansas Real Estate Practice & Procedure Handbook* (4th ed., Kansas Bar Assn. 1999). Available on LexisNexis.

Don F. Dagenais et al., *Examining and Resolving Title Issues* (Natl. Bus. Inst. 2006).

Gregory M. Garvin et al., *Real Estate Law: Advanced Issues and Answers* (Natl. Bus. Inst. 2007).

G. Edgar James et al., *Using a Mechanic's Lien to Get Your Money* (Natl. Bus. Inst. 2007).

Ford R. Nelson & Kellee P. Dunn-Walters, *Resolving Real Estate Title Defects* (Natl. Bus. Inst. 2008).

School Law

Robert L. Bezek, *School Law Issues in Kansas* (Natl. Bus. Inst. 2004).

Joseph Custer et al., *Student Liability Issues* (Natl. Bus. Inst. 2007).

Robert Mead et al., *Kansas Special Education Law* (Natl. Bus. Inst. 2004).

Sentencing Guidelines

Kansas Sentencing Guidelines Desk Reference Manual (Kansas Sentencing Commission 2007).

Tax Law

Kansas Tax Reporter: State and Local Taxes (Commerce Clearing House 1982–).

Mark Bughart et al., *Kansas Sales and Use Tax for Manufacturers* (Natl. Bus. Inst. 1999).

Michael L. McCann et al., *Tax and Business Answers for Nonprofits* (Natl. Bus. Inst. 2006).

Trial/Appellate Practice

Kansas Appellate Practice Handbook (4th ed., Kansas Bar Assn. 2007). (KBA Practice Handbook). Available online at www.kscourts.org/kansas-courts/judicial-council/appellate-practice-handbook/default.asp.

Michael A. Barbara, *Lawyer's Guide to Kansas Evidence* (5th ed., West 2007). Available on Westlaw.

Ruth M. Benien et al., *Trying the Automobile Injury Case in Kansas* (Natl. Bus. Inst. 1999).

William Sampson et al., *Kansas Trial Handbook* (2d ed., West 2006). Available on Westlaw.

Workers' Compensation

ABCs of Workers Compensation (Kansas Bar Assn. 1999).

Anton C. Anderson et al., *Workers' Compensation in Kansas* (Natl. Bus. Inst. 1999).

Matthew S. Crowley et al., *Workers' Compensation Hearings: Techniques and Strategies for Success* (Natl. Bus. Inst. 2006).

Glenn S. Grayson et al., *Kansas Labor and Employment Law* (Natl. Bus. Inst. 1999).

Tom Hammond et al., *Kansas Worker's Compensation Practice Manual* (4th ed., Kansas Bar Assn. 1998 with 2000 Supp.) (KBA Practice Handbook). Available on LexisNexis.

Note. A significant part of this appendix was part of another book chapter by Joseph Custer entitled *Kansas Practice Materials: A Selective Annotated Bibliography*, which was part of the *State Practice Materials: Annotated Bibliographies* monograph published by Hein Publishing in 2002.

About the Authors

Joseph A. Custer, JD, MLIS, is the Associate Director and an Assistant Professor of Law Library at the University of Kansas School of Law, Wheat Law Library.

Christopher L. Steadham, JD, MLIM, is the Faculty Services & Research Librarian at the University of Kansas School of Law, Wheat Law Library.

Index